PRAISE FOR *DIVERSITY, INCLUSION AND BELONGING IN COACHING*

I believe allyship is key to achieving an inclusive society with diversity, equity and belonging, and coaching is, most probably, the best tool to achieve it. I found this book very inspiring, engaging and thought-provoking. A must-read for all practitioners and beneficiaries of coaching.

Dr Riza Kadilar, President, EMCC Global

Salma's new book for me is a 'meta response' to the challenge of diversity, inclusion, equity and belonging. This book brings to the fore the importance of evolving coaching and as a result will no doubt deliver a meta response to the world of coaching.

Claire Camara, Global Chief People Officer, Mediacom

Salma Shah has achieved that sweet spot where you will increase your understanding of coaching and inclusion in equal measure. Both practical and deep, it's delivered with empathy and power and will leave its mark, whether you are new to either discipline or an experienced practitioner.

Rachel Billington, Head of Equity, Diversity and Inclusion (ED&I), AECOM

Timely, challenging, compassionate. An important and essential read for those seeking to play a meaningful role in creating a diverse and inclusive workplace and society. This courageous book explains how understanding our own stories and vulnerabilities, as well as those of our clients, is critical for transformational change. It provides practical tools, useful models, self-reflection and insightful lived experience in a way that is both accessible and engaging.

Dr Tim Spackman, Head of Organisational Development, Skipton Building Society

If I said I could give you a tool that would raise your cultural competence, teach you how to apply it to those who need it most and develop yourself as an emotionally intelligent, nuanced leader with one book, what would you say? This book does all of that and should be required reading for anyone with leadership aspirations.

Hermann Trepesch, Global Diversity and Inclusion, Sanofi

This book is a game-changer within the diversity, inclusion, and belonging (DIB) space. If you are passionate about driving diversity, embedding inclusion, and creating a sense of belonging, this is the only book you need. Whether you are a beginner or an experienced leader I am confident you will benefit hugely. Combining DIB with coaching has the power to inspire people and transform workplaces. If you don't know where to start, start with this book – cover to cover, it's an engaging read.

Zaheer Ahmad MBE, Global Head of Diversity, Equity and Inclusion, GSK

A comprehensive, practical guide for leaders, coaches or for anyone interested in connecting with people on a human level. This book tackles key topics including intersectionality, culture and allyship interwoven with coaching conversations, reflection points and thought-provoking case studies. Drawing on her life experience and coaching skills, Salma has written an insightful approach supporting others to make a deeper connection with their own identity and life experience, whilst expanding their awareness when leading and coaching others.

Tali Shlomo, Inclusion and Diversity Consultant Vice President EMEA, Swiss Re

This book provides a chance for everyone to experience the quality coaching Salma teaches, exploring the techniques and theories, but also providing confidence in exploring challenging topics and the lived experience with our coachees. I thoroughly recommend this book and Salma's work, which is perfectly timed and placed to make a significant difference to so many people's lives.

Mark Laine-Toner, Finance Director, Hermes

This is a hugely timely and nuanced gem of a book. Whilst Salma doesn't shy away from the big issues, she is a gentle and wise companion, acknowledging that we're all fragile and prone to bias. Through illuminating case studies, insights, practice tips and reflection prompts, she encourages, inspires and supports readers to meet people where they truly are and be better professionals and fellow humans in the process.

Liz Hall, editor of Coaching at Work magazine and author of Mindful Coaching

A great invitation to dig deeper into what it really means to be an inclusive coach along with practical steps to unlock personal growth in yourself and others through the lens of the lived experience. Essential reading.

Ash Schofield, CEO, GiffGaff

A critical and ground-breaking text accessible to all leaders on how to use coaching as an enabler for creating and sustaining inclusive, equitable and diverse organizations. Salma explores human connectedness and shared lived experience through the systemic lens with expertise, authenticity and compassion, whilst equipping the reader with insights and practical strategies to apply both individually and systemically for change.

Charmaine Kwame, National Lead for Coaching and Mentoring, NHS England

Diversity, Inclusion and Belonging in Coaching

A practical guide

Salma Shah

Publisher's note

Every possible effort has been made to ensure that the information contained in this book is accurate at the time of going to press, and the publishers and authors cannot accept responsibility for any errors or omissions, however caused. No responsibility for loss or damage occasioned to any person acting, or refraining from action, as a result of the material in this publication can be accepted by the editor, the publisher, or the author.

First published in Great Britain and the United States in 2022 by Kogan Page Limited

Apart from any fair dealing for the purposes of research or private study, or criticism or review, as permitted under the Copyright, Designs and Patents Act 1988, this publication may only be reproduced, stored or transmitted, in any form or by any means, with the prior permission in writing of the publishers, or in the case of reprographic reproduction in accordance with the terms and licences issued by the CLA. Enquiries concerning reproduction outside these terms should be sent to the publishers at the undermentioned addresses:

2nd Floor, 45 Gee Street	8 W 38th Street, Suite 902	4737/23 Ansari Road
London	New York, NY 10018	Daryaganj
EC1V 3RS	USA	New Delhi 110002
United Kingdom		India

www.koganpage.com

Kogan Page books are printed on paper from sustainable forests.

© Salma Shah, 2022

The right of Salma Shah to be identified as the author of this work has been asserted by her in accordance with the Copyright, Designs and Patents Act 1988.

ISBNs

Hardback   978 1 3986 0455 1
Paperback   978 1 3986 0450 6
Ebook   978 1 3986 0454 4

British Library Cataloguing-in-Publication Data

A CIP record for this book is available from the British Library.

Library of Congress Control Number

2022003044

Typeset by Integra Software Services, Pondicherry
Print production managed by Jellyfish
Printed and bound by CPI Group (UK) Ltd, Croydon CR0 4YY

*This book is for my wonderful, witty and wise daughter Mikaila
and
in loving memory of my parents Shah Mohammed
and Khalida Nasreen*

CONTENTS

FOREWORD

Every coaching and mentoring relationship is diverse – they just differ in the degree and the nature of difference. Most of the press about diversity in coaching and mentoring has been focussed on gender, race and culture, but increasing attention is now coming upon areas such as neurodiversity. After 20 years of working with people on the autistic spectrum, learning how their sensory brains see the world through very different lenses, I was lucky enough to encounter a coach with Asperger's syndrome, who opened my eyes to the benefits of having a different experience of the world. I've also formed an interest in what is in some respects the opposite end of the spectrum from Asperger's and autism – highly sensitive persons or HSPs. They, too, can bring a whole new set of perspectives and insights that are filtered out by the efficient neurotypical brain, which dampens down sensory input and is highly selective in what it chooses to notice[1].

An analogy that I have found helpful is to imagine that you were able to see in infra-red. What new perspectives on the world would that give you? You would, for example, be able to sense other people's internal states by the changes in their skin temperature. Which of your current senses (there are 32 of them currently known to science) would you trade for this one?

It's a human instinct to normalise around ourselves. For example, if you ask a typical manager to describe what a good leader is like, they will tend to describe themselves. Which is one very good reason for not placing the identification of future leadership talent in people's bosses! This narrowness of perspective is already giving way in organisations, where the leadership is increasingly vested not in a single, heroic figure, but in the team. The advantage the team brings is its diversity of perspective, which leads to more considered, more balanced decisions and actions.

For many years, the world of coaching and mentoring could have been said to be struggling to keep up. I find coaching theory and practice are dominated by cultural assumptions from the United States, with some influences from Europe – largely ignoring the wealth of wisdom and contextual knowledge of other cultures. Professional coaches have tended to be very similar to their clients. The biggest division in who gets coaching is economic diversity – you have to be able to afford it. I dream that in due course every coach will see how, if they actively engage with diversity, it will enhance their practice.

In Southern Africa, the term *ubuntu* means "I am because we are". I take that as a starting point for the observation that we cannot truly be ourselves if we do not appreciate the differences in others. Whenever I encounter a different way of thinking or interpreting the world, it enriches my understanding of my own history, culture and identity.

For coaches and mentors to embrace diversity fully, we need to develop the skills of observing our own lived experience, our own culture and the limitations and boundaries we place on our own ways of seeing the world and the people, who inhabit it with us. We need to link their narratives with our narratives, in mutual discovery. It is a personal journey that will be different for each of us. We can choose to take that journey with our eyes and ears closed, or to be constantly looking out of the window and conversing with our fellow passengers. Salma Shah's account of her personal journey is a great example for all coaches, who want to engage fully with the wonders of the human diversity that surrounds us.

David Clutterbuck

Endnote

1 One of my current projects is to mentor Asperger's and HSP coaches to describe and compare their experiences in a book.

ACKNOWLEDGEMENTS

Writing this book surprisingly proved both cathartic and more rewarding than I could have ever imagined. None of this would have been possible without the support and generosity of Liz Hall and Lucy Carter at Kogan Page. Some people, the right people walk into your life and turn the lights on. Eternally grateful to Katherine Chowdry, Joanne Cook, Sukhy Bains and Kevin Lyons for their backing and encouragement.

A very special thanks to my pioneer coaches who took a leap of faith as we came together during the first lockdown in the 2020 to launch MYP coach training. You will always have a very special place in this work. Abdul Rob, Amer Khan, Basirat Agboola, Emma Ferres, Erin Ashley, Jas Deogan, Lakhveer Singh, Nathan Watson, Nazreen Visram, Ritu Sharma and Susana Fernandes. Also, I appreciate the courage and generosity of all those who shared their lived experience for the case studies.

This book wouldn't have finished on time without the deadlines, patience and encouragement from my development editor Anne-Marie Heeney. Elias Niazi for cups of tea and stepping in on the domestic front during the final edits while I nursed a fractured shoulder. Harriet Assem for hosting millions of playdates so I could get on with the writing, and listening patiently to my writer's angst with Uvie Peile as each chapter unfolded.

My lovely friends who regularly checked in to remind me to switch off and have fun - Deborah Maguire, Fiona Cambriopolous and Hema Shah.

I also want to thank my younger brother Inam Shah who has always had my back and has taught me the true meaning of integrity, generosity and abundance. For keeping things real and believing in me whole-heartedly, championing and supporting me unconditionally. I am so lucky to have you in my life.

Finally, to all my family, friends and colleagues who are part of my lived experience.

Introduction

I'd like to begin with an experience I had with a coaching client. Karan worked for a large multi-national computer technology company and had been promoted into a new leadership position managing a team of sales representatives. It was his first time leading a team and he was struggling to find his feet. Prior to his promotion he had been the highest quota-achieving sales representative in his department. The vice president of his division had spotted his potential and wanted to give him the best opportunity to succeed. Following our coaching 'chemistry' session, to establish if we were a good fit, we both agreed that we would like to work together. Karan emphatically let me know he wasn't a fan of fluffy conversations and had a clear preference for rational scientific-backed evidence. I had a sense that he didn't really buy into the idea of coaching.

Karan's appearance was professional and he was well-dressed in a navy suit. I found myself warming to his slightly quirky side, with his trendy bright yellow sports watch and coordinated matching yellow notebook. My curiosity was alive and ready to go. Over the years I had coached many senior leaders from the same organization and on paper Karan was no different. He was in his early 40s, a father of two, with all the responsibilities of juggling the priorities of a very demanding corporate career and carving out precious time for family life.

Within a few coaching sessions, I started to notice a familiar pattern. At the beginning of each coaching session, as we agreed the outcomes for our hour together, Karan would typically offer a sanitized textbook management issue he wanted to work on. These would include time management or work prioritization, and we would unpick around the edges for a short time. Then following his lead, and a few powerful questions from my side, we would move on to his insecurities and deep-rooted fears. The real issue we unsurfaced was rarely the same topic we had agreed at the beginning and yet transformational and deep.

As the coaching sessions progressed, it became evident that from Karan's perspective his immediate boss, who was also new to the organization, didn't rate his ability or trust him. He felt she was watching him like a hawk, waiting for him to mess things up so she could remove him from the team. According to him, she already had chosen her favourites and had pretty much written him off. He had an inkling he was not being invited to crucial meetings and deliberately being set up to fail. He increasingly felt excluded from important decisions, isolated and even started to question whether he belonged in the organization or the technology sector as a whole.

As Karan's trust in me grew, he started to open up and show vulnerability about how he was really feeling in his new role. He also revealed how his family and cultural background had a huge impact on how he saw himself at work. His parents had emmigrated to the UK from India and had run the local newspaper shop until retiring a few years ago. Their working day started at 4 am and finished at 10 pm, seven days a week. There wasn't much quality time for family life. Karan was very close to his sister, who had married and moved away to Singapore. Feeling isolated, and that he didn't belong, was a familiar, painful emotional trigger.

As a newly appointed manager, this promotion was his big break and he desperately wanted to succeed. He didn't want to let down the Vice President, his family or himself. Yet the stress of feeling that he didn't fit in or belong with the wider leadership team was overwhelming. Strong emotions were surfacing and his destructive inner voice was judging, belittling and critical. Once we started to further explore his inner critic, Karan started to open up about how isolating it felt to be the only person who looked like him through school, university and now his working career. He felt that, despite doing well academically, he always felt he had to work harder to fit in; that he was feeling burnout, sick and tired of work politics. How he wanted to be a great role model for his children so that they could be at ease with their identity and their rightful place in society.

Through our work together Karan progressively felt he could voice what he was feeling at a deeper level. Our coaching together meant he felt psychologically safe to be authentically seen and heard. The sessions would weave in and out of joining the dots of his lived experience, of having the confidence to name how it felt to be from an under-represented group in a large multi-national corporation: conquering his inner critic and what he needed to do to be successful. The coaching was not about fixing or analysing the past. However, once 'named' by him, to ignore his cultural identity, experiences and background would have been a huge missed opportunity for the deeper transformational work.

My coaching experience with Karan was profound. The fact that we both were born in the UK to immigrant parents and had a South Asian heritage was purely coincidental. I was mindful about not colluding with his immigrant story of belonging, inclusion and fitting in. I had to be careful not to fall into the trap of projecting my personal deeper feelings and aligning our experiences too closely in our coaching relationship. By giving voice to his lived experience meant that he felt seen and heard. It meant he could reframe and normalize his current challenges in the wider context of his life story. Karan went on to lead his team to success, got promoted again and joined a different manager (who he respected) in the same organization. Last time we spoke he proudly shared he had been headhunted and was now very happily working for a competitor.

There are three key points I hope you'll extract from Karan's story:

- The emotional scripts around belonging and inclusion have many layers of visible and invisible complexities for all of us and specifically for those of us from under-represented groups. To be seen and heard is transformational and healing.

- As a coach, manager or leader, it is our privilege if our client or team member feels safe and trusting enough to share what is truly happening for them. Understanding the context of the client from a wider systemic lens allows us to be more effective as coaches.

- Who we are as a coach, and how we show up, has a huge impact in creating psychological safety and a safe space for our client to be seen and their lived experience to be heard.

In this book, my focus is on guiding coaches and managers with tools and knowledge to build their skills to support and coach through a wider lens of inclusion, belonging, equity and diversity.

When working with someone who is very different, we may get drawn in to playing it safe and lose confidence to ask powerful and challenging questions. I want you to have the skills and ability to be fully conscious and create spontaneous relationships with all your clients, employing a style that is open, flexible and confident.

Thank you for joining me here.

Terminology

Language, like the society we live in, is constantly evolving. With this in mind, in this book I will both generally and in case studies use the traditional pronouns *he* and *she*, and in recognition of non-binary gender identification, I also use *they*. I use the term *under-represented group* to describe a community that makes up a smaller percentage than a large subgroup within a population. This includes a group that is less represented in one subset (eg, employees in a particular sector, such as IT) than in the general population, and may refer to gender, social class, race/ethnicity, physical or mental ability, LGBTQ+ status and many more.

My ultimate goal is well-intentioned and my primary endeavour is to approach this work from a place of deep respect and kindness.

Confidentiality

From the perspective of the people I have coached, and the generosity of those who have shared their stories, where necessary I have modified characteristics that would reveal their identity. I've changed names and, in some cases, places, organizations and the sectors in which they work. The essence of their stories remains intact.

We are both fragile and biased

We all have fragility

In writing this book I decided to run a poll through the social media platform of LinkedIn. The poll question was as follows:

'While there are many conversations happening about diversity and inclusion in the workplace, I know that some people feel uncomfortable talking about it freely. What do you feel holds people back from talking about inclusion, diversity and belonging in their workplace?'

Fear of saying the wrong thing	76 per cent
Lack of knowledge	16 per cent
Lack of confidence	8 per cent

The result was not at all a surprise as it echoed many conversations I've had with coaches, colleagues, friends and family in recent times: an overwhelming fear of saying the wrong thing; worry that we may unintentionally be offensive or cause hurt. The seismic shifts of major events such as COVID-19 and the Black Lives Matter protests mean our lives and our workplaces will never be the same again. Both these events have affected different segments of the population differently.

Coaching the lived experience through a wider systemic lens of inclusion, belonging, equity and diversity is crucial to serving a diverse population. However, in order to take this big step forward we need to acknowledge our own fragility. Our fear of getting it wrong. Every single one of us in some way or other is fragile. The aim of this book is to give you the understanding and tools to have those courageous coaching conversations.

We all have bias

We all face a fundamental paradox. We are inherently social and wired to connect. Getting along with one another is important to our survival as human beings. Nonetheless, we are also hardwired to spot and react to differences, and we often do so without really being aware of doing so or how it informs our initial perceptions of each other. These are our unconscious biases at work.

The term *implicit bias* (also described as unconscious bias) first entered the mainstream in 1995 by psychologists Greenwald and Banaji, who presented the idea that our social behaviour is predominantly influenced by unconscious associations and social judgements. Cognitive scientists have named several biases that frequently occur in all of us. For example, apparently the first two things we generally notice when we meet someone new is their skin colour and gender. Perszyk et al found that children as young as four years of age demonstrate implicit and explicit bias at the intersection of race and gender (2019). This instinctive evolutionary bias is linked to our survival and whether or not we are in any danger. However, we also have learnt bias which we absorb throughout our lives from society, media, education, family, friends and so on.

As coaches we need to be aware and mindful of both our instinctive and learnt biases, and how they impact how we show up as a coach, our behaviour, our presence, verbal and non-verbal communication. We must accept that the quality of the coaching experience can be impacted by our biases.

Here is a question for you: is it more effective to work with a coach from a similar cultural and/or professional background?

Over the years the answer to this question has led to a heated debate between coaches, with both sides providing evidence of their experience.

Is the question emotionally triggering? If so, I invite you to reflect on why you feel emotionally triggered.

Next, let's consider this statement: we need to take positive action in offering professional coach training to people from under-represented groups.

WHAT ARE YOUR THOUGHTS?

Most likely your response to both these questions will have elements of your personal confirmation bias. This is the tendency to discount or disregard information that disagrees with our assumptions, even if there are well-proven facts to the contrary and in spite of any risks associated with doing so. It can happen if we are too quick to draw conclusions and make assumptions without fully exploring the details of a situation, and stop actively listening without fully understanding. Confirmation bias is one of the most challenging ones as it takes time and commitment to overturn.

I strongly believe as coaches, leaders and learners if we are going to deep dive into coaching through this wider lens we need to reflect on our own biases and fears. Especially if we want to create trust on both sides and the psychological safety for our clients to bring their lived experience into the coaching space.

What do I mean by the lived experience?

Lived experience means you have lived something personally. It is subjective; it is not something you can be taught, can learn or can pass on through relationships with others. It is not something you argue; it is something you have. Only those who have experienced the phenomena can communicate them to the outside world. It therefore provides an understanding of an experience from those who have lived it.

We need to recognize and accept the complexities of the lived stories of our clients and that there are systemic inequalities that our clients may have experienced and which we cannot single-handedly change. As coaches we must simultaneously always stay focused on the present and the things we can influence and control, while appreciating the reality of the lived experience of under-represented groups.

Before we move to the next section, let's look at a few facts. The list below is not exhaustive. I just want you to stop and absorb the impact of a handful examples of inequality for under-represented groups.

- Black pregnant women are statically five times more likely to die at childbirth. (MBRRACE-UK, 2019)

- Over half of autistic people (60 per cent), dyspraxic people (55 per cent) and dyscalculic people (53 per cent) reported that other people in their workplace behave in a way that excludes neurodivergent colleagues. But this feeling is not entirely shared by their neurotypical colleagues, with only 29 per cent agreeing that this is the case. (Institute of Leadership and Management, 2020)

- Young black males in London are 19 times more likely to be stopped and searched by police. (UCL study, 2020)

- Figures from the UK Home Office show that anti-LGBTQ+ hate crimes have been on the rise for two years running. Figures published in October 2020 revealed that sexual orientation hate crimes increased 19 per cent (to 15,835) over the previous year. Hate crimes against trans people increased by 16 per cent (to 2,450) over the previous year.

- A study by UCL Institute of Education (IOE) found that 46 per cent of all schools in England have no teachers from under-represented groups and, even in ethnically diverse schools, they are under-represented in senior leadership positions.

- White males from low-income families are the 'least likely' group to go to university (Department for Education).

Whereas diversity refers to all the many ways that people differ, equity is about fairness of opportunity. The examples demonstrate a need to understand the barriers faced by these groups and an appreciation of their lack of opportunity. It's about acknowledging we need to create and tend to a fair playing field, to use a familiar metaphor. This should translate to taking courageous action and treating everyone differently based on their needs.

Many people from under-represented groups tell me time and time again how they have felt innocently 'shut down' by their coach and didn't feel safe enough to really share what they were feeling. Or they had a 'gut feeling' the coach wouldn't really understand what it was like to be in their shoes, so they avoided certain areas or accepted that the coaching was an ok(ish) superficial experience. This may feel uncomfortable to read as a coach. These conversations made me reflect about my experience of coaching Karan and the deep connection we had made which allowed him to share his lived experience.

A question that many people may have considered is: how do you effectively coach someone whose culture, sexual identity, religious belief, social class, ancestral history, language and family background are very different from yours?

From my experience, one of the unique aspects of coaching is its ability to meet people where they are. Coaching the lived experience is recognizing that as coaches we need to be curious, responsive and open to much more than what the client is actually saying. We also need to be present to what they see, think and feel and how they react to the world around them. The fact is that our lived experience is essentially private and delicate.

When working with someone who is very different from us, we may get drawn into playing it safe and lose our nerve to ask powerful, gritty and challenging questions. Our presence as a coach is the ability to be fully conscious and create a spontaneous relationship with the client, employing a style that is open, flexible and confident.

This book will support and guide you along your journey to have those powerful coaching conversations.

About this book

This book provides a model for coaching the lived experience. Many coaches and consultants feel unskilled and ill-equipped to work with a client's deeper personal story. Bridging the gap between where we are and where we want and need to be requires effort, reflection and learning together.

Now more than ever, understanding how to coach through a wider systemic lens of inclusion, belonging and diversity is going to be one of the critical tools for supporting and making a positive impact – a crucial asset in the multi-layered complexities that coaches, organizations, leaders and teams are going to face in their new expanded role.

Coaching through this lens is how you should do everything and is not a separate area of work. My coach training programme, Mastering

Your Power, has the golden thread of Inclusion, Belonging, Equity and Diversity threaded throughout it. It is not tagged on as an afterthought or, worst case, a tick in the box exercise.

Although I do refer to under-represented groups in this book, I want to be clear that this work is for everyone. It is inclusive. Being inclusive is not being scared to turn everything on its head to see a different point of view and creating a bit of chaos. It's about being open to putting ourselves into an uncomfortable situation; recognizing that for many of us who are from under-represented groups we may feel constantly 'other' and uncomfortable.

The book will cover the following areas:

- Lived experience;
- Identification;
- Inclusion;
- Belonging;
- Entanglements;
- Trauma;
- Resilience;
- Psychological safety;
- Thriving;
- Equity;
- Authenticity.

The work here is about understanding the behaviour, thoughts and emotions of our client within a larger context of culture, religious belief, class and socio-economic realities, not just the content of their coaching scenario or issue. It's the recognition that learning is happening at an individual level and in dynamic engagement with a wider system.

To coach through this wider lens, you need to develop inclusive and expansive coaching skills and presence. Among other things, you need to be open-heartedly curious and empathetic to the inequities and inequalities of those from under-represented groups. You also need to be skilled at understanding strong emotions. You will need emotional intelligence and awareness; the ability to navigate your emotions and the wisdom to recognize strong emotions in others and navigate their emotions too. Give yourself the permission to be clumsy. Be prepared to do the work to build mutual trust.

Getting the most out of this book

Each chapter will prompt you about different aspects which will have influenced and shaped the lived experience of both yourself as coach and your client. In the rush of our daily lives, we do not consciously examine or unravel the layers which are impacting how we experience the world, how we behave and subsequently the issues that our clients face.

The intention for this book is as follows:

- Inform and establish the contour of the lived experience.
- Offer you an opportunity to reflect on the principles of how to coach through a wider lens of inclusion, belonging, equity and diversity.
- Prompt you to dig deeper and reflect on the content of each chapter.
- Offer guidance and tools for powerful coaching.

To get the most from this book it is important to remain open-minded and empathetic. Reflect on the emotions that are triggered and, if it helps, do the exercises in a pair or as part of a group.

Who is this book for?

This book is for leaders, coaches, trainers and consultants who are committed to playing their part in creating a diverse, equitable and inclusive society. It's for those who are ready to acknowledge that there are systemic realities of inequity and privilege. It is important to note here that there are no quick-fix shortcuts to this work. Yes, you will learn tools and techniques; however, the real work is examining ourselves and looking inward to identify where and who we want to be as a leader and a coach.

This book is also for those who use coaching as a tool to partner with someone in a thought-provoking and creative process that inspires them to maximize their personal potential; those who are now ready to go deeper with their coaching practice. It's for all kinds of coaches internal, external, life, transformational, executive and so on.

It is for coaches and leaders who have only just started to dip their toes into conversations around belonging, inclusion, equity and diversity. For those of us who have a lot more experience and knowledge in this area, you may find some of the content familiar and other sections new and informative. For some, this book will be emotionally triggering. The work in this area is ongoing. To quote Socrates, 'The more I learn, the less I realize I know'.

About me

Sharing our stories is important so that we can change attitudes.

> I tell my story, not because it is unique, but because it is not. It is the story of many girls. (Malala Yousafzai, Nobel Peace Prize Lecture, 2014)

This work would be incomplete without the personal stories and experiences. It is important to know ourselves and how our lived experience and identity have shaped our perspective. To honour the work that I am asking you to do I will share some of my lived story with you too.

The Partition in 1947 was the division of British India into two independent states, India and Pakistan, displacing between 10 and 20 million people along religious lines and creating an overwhelming refugee crisis. My grandparents, and my parents as small children, were also displaced and uprooted from their homes – moving to Pakistan. Our ancestral home is still a disputed area of Kashmir. Kashmir is known as paradise on Earth, and it has been ranked as the world's second-most romantic destination, only next to Switzerland. Towards the end of their lives in the UK, my parents yearned to visit their homeland, Kashmir, one more time – sadly this remained an unrequited longing. The story of migration, struggle and feeling that we don't belong is a deep-rooted ancestral story.

In 1963, in his mid-20s, my late father arrived in the UK from Pakistan with just £5 in his back pocket and the address of a distant contact in Halifax. A very kind Sikh man who worked at Heathrow airport spotted my dad looking somewhat lost at arrivals and offered him a bed and a meal for the night at his home in Hounslow, west London before dropping him off at the coach station and onwards to Halifax. According to my parents, during those early waves of immigration to the UK, strangers with a similar background randomly looked out for and helped each other. Although my father and the Sikh man were of different religious backgrounds, they both spoke Punjabi and had a shared cultural identity.

Halifax was a short stay and he eventually ended up in Reading, Berkshire in a shared small Edwardian terraced house with three of my uncles. My late mother joined him from Pakistan two years later and I was born two years after her arrival.

Our shared terraced house was home to four other families, all uncles, aunties and cousins, and was very close to Reading University's campus. Years later, my mother told me that while she would push the one-year-old me in my pram up and down Donnington Gardens where we lived, she would look at the students from Reading University and dream that I too one day would go to Reading University. Going to university was a big deal in those days. Little did she know then that is exactly where I would end up 18 years later. What happened in between those 18 years is just one chapter of my lived experience that I will share with you next.

The UK at that time was in the swing of flower power, mini-skirts and free love. I can only guess the culture shock for my parents, as the Pakistan they left behind was, and still is in contrast, a very conservative country.

At the age of five, for a number of reasons, my parents decided to move to Bolton, a former mill town in north-west England, historically and traditionally a part of Lancashire. Our first Bolton home was a two-up, two-down terrace, with an outside toilet and no bathroom. People in those days would go to the local swimming bath to have a shower. Instead, we converted the coal shed to a very rustic indoor washroom with a tap and bucket. In years to come this proved useful for acclimatizing to the experience of camping.

My parents took a shine to the Northern warmth and friendliness. My school, Clarendon Primary, in the 1970s was multi-cultural and my time there was innocent and happy. I was one of the clever ones and knew it. The school was mostly a mix of white working class, Gujarati Hindu and Gujarati Muslim children of Indian heritage. We (as in myself, my brothers and my cousins) were in the minority as British Pakistanis. We thought we were rather special and proud to be different. The seeds of being different and sticking out were sown very early on. Also, what really stood us apart was that our parents were heavily invested in our education and didn't really want us to mix too much with the other children.

Passing my 11-plus exam was a big deal, yet my time at Deane Grammar school was miserable. There were very few Asian children in my class and no Muslim girls in the whole school; I just didn't fit in. I can recall conversations with a friend at the age of 12 who would often tell me proudly that, according to Hitler, people like her who had blonde hair and blue eyes were a superior race to other skin colours. She was a kind person and I figured her comments were ignorant rather than racist. However, I could also see that in her eyes she believed she was superior to me. Inwardly enraged, I swallowed what she said and decided to let it go but the fact I am writing about it now is evidence that her words hurt and lingered for a lot longer.

Furthermore, my grammar school was in an average middle-class area of Bolton and it was the first time I became aware that we didn't live in the posh part of the town. A handful of mean, privileged boys in my class took great delight at making cruel jibes about the area I came from. They weren't aimed at me, yet I took their comments personally. At school, I rarely spoke in big groups and overnight lost all my confidence.

As I had hit puberty, my parents were by now very strict about how I dressed and what I did. My only refuge out of the house was to go the library with my younger brother as a chaperone. I was excluded from parties, school trips, out-of-school activities and sport – actually most of what I would now describe as teenage life. I withdrew into a shell, only to resurface when I started university several years later.

By this time my home life was equally miserable. My mother was a seamstress, working from home from 6 am to midnight, on a shockingly illegal low hourly rate. My father would work six days a week, twelve hours a day as a welder. He would constantly be in a bad mood and have burns from the flames at work on his arms and legs. His idea of a holiday was to do DIY around the house and rope us all in. Our lives were all about hard work and surviving, with no time or space for thriving and fun. The positive thing was that our lives were very stable, with a lot of structure and sensible routines.

Reflecting back on my early life, my parents were both probably traumatized to some degree by the sheer weight on their shoulders of the pressure of building a life in a new country, sending money back to family in Pakistan and raising children in a culture which was alien to their values. Growing up in Britain in the 1970s and 80s, we were terrified of the far-right National Front. Racist graffiti, telling people like us to go home, was commonplace. We were regularly reminded that we didn't belong. School didn't feel psychologically safe and out in the street we were always on high alert in case a racist thug happened to cross our path.

Fast-forward to university and I was fortunate with good grades to escape the shackles of strict parents. At Reading University, I made friends from all over the world and the UK too, most of whom I'm still in contact with. It was by far the happiest time of my life and a real turning point. The fact that I was probably the only British Pakistani on my course and in my hall of residence didn't bother me. I was by now very used to being the only person who looks like me and ok with it.

After graduation, I fell into a relatively successful career in the technology sector. Again, I was the only Asian in my department and beyond. By now I was living an independent life in London and doing my best to blend in with my colleagues. I was authentic in that I stuck to my core values, however, fitting in was important to getting on at work. As Pakistan was often in the news for all the wrong reasons I would downplay my family background and, for a while, I even told people that we were originally from India as that felt much cooler.

One time I was working late when the office cleaners had arrived and were vacuuming around me. The cleaner assigned to my desk area was an older Punjabi lady. I knew she was Punjabi by her clothes as she was wearing the traditional shalwar kameez. I hadn't really noticed her before but, on this occasion, I looked up from my desk to see her smiling at me and our eyes met. In Punjabi she shyly asked, 'Do you work here too, with all these people?' I replied in Punjabi that yes, I did. Her smile broke into a wide grin and she told me how happy she was to see one of 'us' in a nice job like this.

This experience has stayed with me and meant more and more over the years, as I've grieved over losing my parents and the legacy of their hard struggles and hard work.

This is only a fraction of my lived experience and story. I will be sharing more throughout the book. My story so far is based around culture, belonging and identity. I'm also fully aware of the other strands of diversity and have much more to share from a variety of lenses.

I want you to squeeze as much value as you possibly can from this book. Start with Chapter 1 – Lived Experience and follow this with Chapter 2 – Identification. After this you may choose to continue reading the book sequentially or, if you're feeling a tug to a particular chapter, follow your intuition and dive in.

Take your time to reflect on the questions after each chapter. Your learning will deepen as you read along. We also learn through connecting with others and sharing our experiences. You may want to buddy up with a friend or another coach and discuss what is coming up for you while you work through the chapters and the reflective exercises.

It is OK to be clumsy

As I mentioned earlier, I give you permission to get it wrong and in return I ask for your forgiveness if I get something wrong. We all have limitations and blind spots. My knowledge is imperfect and if I waited for that moment of perfection this book would never get written. Writing this book has gripped me with fear, as much as when I first started to express what had been bubbling up in me for a while: that we need diversity of coaches; both diversity of thought and diversity in terms of more coaches from under-represented groups. We need to understand the complexity of the lived experience of those from under-represented groups.

At times, you may find this book challenging and uncomfortable. You may even feel triggered. For those from a majority group there may be discomfort as themes of privilege and inequity surface. For those from an under-represented group, the book will bring to the surface traumas related to past experience just as writing the introduction has for me. Remember that we are all fragile and we all have bias; it's how we use this awareness that will make a difference.

Before you start

Spend some time reflecting on and journaling the following questions:

- Why are you reading this book?
- What thoughts have been triggered as you read the introduction?
- How did this make you feel?
- How will this book improve your life?
- What would you like to see change in the world today?
- What part do you want to play in that change?

References

Corry, K (2020) 'London's most deprived neighbourhoods see more stop and searches', UCL, December, https://www.ucl.ac.uk/news/2020/dec/londons-most-deprived-neighbourhoods-see-more-stop-and-searches (archived at https://perma.cc/BH68-S9H2)

Coughlan, S (2020) 'The "taboo" about who doesn't go to university', BBC, September https://www.bbc.co.uk/news/education-54278727 (archived at https://perma.cc/QT8F-536R)

Greenwald, A G and Banaji, M R (1995) Implicit social cognition: Attitudes, self-esteem, and stereotypes, *Psychological Review,* 102 (1), 4–27

Institute of Leadership and Management (2020) 'Half of all leaders and managers would not employ a neurodivergent person', http://www.institutelm.com/resourceLibrary/half-of-all-leaders-and-managers-would-not-employ-a-neurodivergent-person1.html (archived at https://perma.cc/VZ6W-HFDJ)

Perszyk, D, Lei R F, Bodenhausen, G V and Richeson, J A (2019) Bias at the intersection of race and gender: Evidence from preschool-aged children, *Developmental Science* 22 (3):e12788 DOI:10.1111/desc.12788 https://spcl.yale.edu/sites/default/files/files/Perszyk_et_al-2019-Developmental_Science.pdf (archived at https://perma.cc/S28Z-2FCG)

UCL (2020) '46% of all schools in England have no BAME teachers', December, https://www.ucl.ac.uk/ioe/news/2020/dec/46-all-schools-england-have-no-bame-teachers (archived at https://perma.cc/3K82-L5QT)

UK Home Office (2020) 'Hate crime, England and Wales, 2019 to 2020', October, https://www.gov.uk/government/statistics/hate-crime-england-and-wales-2019-to-2020/hate-crime-england-and-wales-2019-to-2020 (archived at https://perma.cc/QM4Y-37J6)

Yousafzai, M (2014) Nobel Peace Prize Lecture, December, https://www.nobelprize.org/uploads/2018/06/yousafzai-lecture_en.pdf (archived at https://perma.cc/J768-EURE)

01

Coaching the lived experience

Know all the theories, master all the techniques, but as you touch a human soul be just another human soul.

C G JUNG

So often I hear the phrase, 'I tried coaching once but my coach didn't really get me, so I won't bother again'. This is heart breaking as I know from my own experience of coaching and from working with clients the ripple effect of transformational coaching. A powerful coaching session, even in the guise of career coaching, can have a wider impact on someone's family, wider community and socially.

As coaches we need to hold the space for our client through our presence and their safety. Coaching dynamically is often described as 'dancing in the moment', by holding our client's agenda, accessing our intuition and letting our client lead. The question we need to pose is, what kind of dance are we doing? Is it bhangra, ballet or break-dancing (Shah, 2020)?

Coaching is about being in the present and helping the coachee to move forward, yet our lives are a culmination of whispers of past losses too. If there is a wide cultural and systemic difference between the coach and coachee, there is a significant risk that the dance may be one of awkwardness as we avoid stepping on each other's toes. The following example is one demonstration of this.

CASE STUDY: SEEMA

Seema, a talented, emotionally strong and respected senior staff nurse, brought to the coaching session a huge dilemma she was facing. She absolutely loved her work at a leading London hospital but was getting married in a few months. There was a lot of subtle pressure from her fiancé and his family to give up her job. The shift work, and irregular hours, were not considered fitting and acceptable for a future daughter-in-law who would be joining their family system.

For Seema, leaving her nursing career would be heart-wrenching but she felt there was no other choice. Whereas her own family had been accepting of her career decision, her future in-laws were not as supportive.

Over many sessions her coach, following a linear questioning style of coaching model, explored areas such as future self, limiting beliefs, choices, purpose and values. However, it quickly became very clear to Seema that her coach was missing the mark and just didn't understand the depth of her dilemma or what it felt like to be caught up in the different cultural systems of work and family. She also felt that her coach's questioning style was somewhat judgemental about the culture of origin of her in-laws' family and was lacking in empathy. Overall, the session was ok at a superficial level; however, Seema left feeling dejected and not fully seen or heard by her coach.

The dilemma that Seema was facing was more than just complying with her future family's desires. It was deeply rooted in her lived experience of a second-generation immigrant and immersed in the expectations of her future role as the wife of the eldest son in his ancestral family system. Her parents had emigrated to the UK from Sri Lanka in the 1960s and had made many sacrifices to give her the best life they knew. She was torn between conscious and unconscious loyalties to many systems: her ancestors, family, culture, gender and nursing profession. Despite her dream of rising in the ranks of her role and her loyalty and sense of purpose attached to her nursing career, at this time in her life her hidden loyalty and sense of belonging – like a magnetic field – was pulling her in the direction of what she needed to do to belong to her family and cultural system of origin.

In the few months of working with Seema, her coach hadn't truly understood her lived experience, identity or the many systems she belonged to. Unknown to her coach, Seema left the coaching experience feeling disappointed and misunderstood.

What is the lived experience?

Behind every one of us is our lived experience: a childhood, cultural, socio-economic, religious and gender identity and a systemic ancestral story that can inspire us to achieve greatness, act with compassion, be resilient and make a difference. Yet our lived experience can also wreak havoc, cause self-sabotage, contribute towards our playing small and leave us lacking the confidence to be authentic.

Lived experience means you've lived it personally and therefore it is subjective. It isn't something you can be taught, learn or pass on through relationships with others. It isn't something you argue; it's something you have. Only those who have experienced the phenomena can communicate them to the outside world. It therefore provides an understanding of an experience from those who have lived it. There is an entire field of study relating to lived experience of the world: Phenomenology. It's an arena seeking to understand the sense we make of our experience.

Unless you yourself have lived the experience of feeling excluded, rejected, abandoned, not belonging, shamed, abused, bullied, or experienced racism, sexism, microaggressions etc., there is no guarantee as a coach or leader that you will understand the deeper repercussions of these when they show up in a coaching conversation.

The impact of these experiences may often surface in coaching disguised as a lack of confidence, denial, avoidance, anger, fatigue, imposter syndrome, self-sabotage or low self-worth. Sometimes, the impact of negative life experiences may appear in relatively positive or character-building ways: resilience, a heightened sense of vigilance, street savviness, tolerance, inner strength and courage.

With reference to coaching someone from an under-represented minority group, regardless of our individual multi-layered mix of identity, we are too often frozen because we cannot address unfairness that we ourselves do not see or have never experienced. We may lack the courage to ask difficult and powerful questions and fear the potential to do more harm. Or we skirt around the real issue with weak questions and end up inadvertently shutting the client down.

The aim should be to avoid what happened in Seema's case where the coach inadvertently shut down the conversation and Seema left feeling misunderstood and not seen or heard.

The aim of this chapter specifically, and indeed the whole book, is to give you the tools for self-awareness, humility, presence and the courage and confidence to coach someone from a very different background and life experience from yours.

How do you effectively coach someone whose culture, sexual identity, religious belief, social class, ancestral history, language and family background are very different from yours?

At the heart of this work is to acknowledge that being open, empathetic and curious about our client's lived experience and identity

FIGURE 1.1   Mastering your power coaching

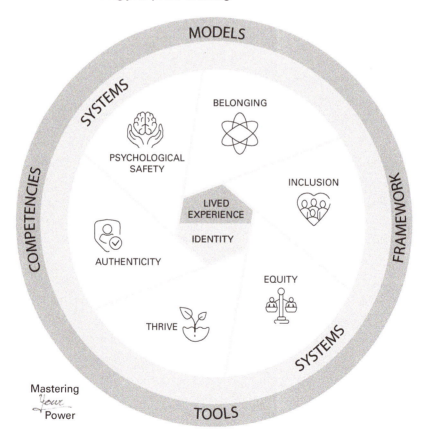

is the key which will unlock the many gated doors to powerful, transformational coaching. In our role as coach, we need to be present, respectful and receptive to our client's sense of belonging, inclusion, equity, psychological safety, ability to thrive and the willingness and permission to be authentic. We all have our personal story related to these areas. However, if you're from an under-represented minority group there is also a very high chance this complexity will be deeper and more complex.

We need to understand, acknowledge and accept the interplay of the complex systems to which our client belongs and the hidden loyalties towards those systems. Just because our client does not mention their loyalty to their cultural system, or the family they belong to, it does not mean that their loyalty is not alive and kicking. Our role as coaches is not to fix their system. Our role is to be present so our client can make powerful choices at the appropriate time. The focus should always be the client's agenda and never that of the coach.

Seema's case study was an example of this. Her lived experience and identity was as a British-born female of Sri-Lankan heritage. Despite her life purpose and passion for nursing and healing the sick, her sense of belonging was firmly rooted in her family of origin and the unwritten rules she had to follow to retain her place in her cultural system and family. Seema had a more powerful hidden loyalty to her family system than her nursing profession. Keeping her future partner's family happy was more important to her at the time as it fed her deeper desire and longing for belonging and inclusion.

This dynamic could change over time because nothing is permanent. A clumsy coaching conversation could close Seema off from reaching out again for coaching if things start to shift and she wants to explore entering the nursing profession again. We have to give ourselves the permission as coaches to ask clumsy questions, but if we are doing the inner work to develop our awareness and widen our coaching lens we are heading in the right direction.

Without understanding the wider lens which is core to the coaching framework in this book (see Figure 1.1 Mastering your power coaching), linear coaching with just the basic recipe of exploring values, purpose, goals and actions may under certain circumstances be too oversimplified and miss the mark. Central to the Mastering Your Power Coaching framework is the coachee's sense of identity and lived experience. There must be a recognition that when coaching someone, especially from an under-represented minority group, the coach needs to have an awareness and curiosity of their client's 'lived experience' of belonging, inclusion, psychological safety, equity, thriving vs surviving and the reality of authenticity. Consider the many systems they are part of: do they feel psychologically safe? Do they feel included? Do they belong? All this and much more will be explored throughout this book.

The transformational coaching experience Seema needed was to support her to find a deeper resolution and acceptance of her inner systemic conflict. In her own time, by understanding the complexity of her lived experience and identity, she may join the nursing profession again. Allowing her to feel psychologically safe enough to accept and say this may take longer than a few coaching sessions; the coach should be aware and understanding of this.

As transformational coaches, alongside developing our skills of coaching someone who is very different from us and particularly someone from an under-represented group, we need to do our own work on our lived experience and identity: our own sense of belonging, inclusion, equity, thriving, psychological safety and authenticity. In this book I will strongly encourage you to do your own reflection work as well as immerse yourself in this new approach to coaching. Doing our own work means we can be more empathetic towards our clients.

I also want you to become mindful of how you get in your own way when it comes to coaching someone from an under-represented group that is very different from yours. Speaking to coaches from under-represented minority groups, the following things are important to them when they themselves are being coached; *some of these may offer you clues about how you might be getting in your own way.*

- Not feeling misunderstood.
- Not feeling rescued.
- Not feeling patronized.
- Not feeling judged.

- Coach needs to understand what I need.
- Quickly being understood.
- Not having to edit what I share during coaching.
- Instant rapport so I can move on to the more uncomfortable questions.
- Cultural similarities.
- An understanding of cultural pressures, nuances which can easily be missed.
- Feeling seen and heard.
- Meaningful coaching vs superficial surface level coaching.
- Not being shut down during the coaching session.
- Coaches' questions are so off the mark that there is an obvious lack of understanding.

Could familiar experiences negatively impact the coaching experience?

There is a popular universal school of thought that as a professional coach you don't need to understand someone's background to do great coaching. There is even an argument that by being too familiar there could be a danger of the coach colluding with the client. Or, if the coach and the client are too similar, the client may not feel comfortable sharing everything through fear of feeling judged by their coach. The perception of feeling judged or misunderstood can have a huge detrimental effect on the coaching experience.

One example of this was Naseem.

CASE STUDY: NASEEM

Naseem is a 35-year-old Muslim professional woman, who had started to wear the hijab a few years earlier but was now questioning if she wanted to continue wearing it. The type of hijab she liked wearing was a colourful stylish silk headscarf which covered her head and neck but left her face clear. Naseem wanted to explore this inner conflict with a coach; however, she feared being judged if the coach was Muslim too. She consciously searched out a non-Muslim coach for help and support.

Naseem first spoke about her dilemma with a non-Muslim coach who, similar to Seema's coach, used a linear coaching model and explored action taking options around reaching out to the Imam (spiritual and religious leader) at her local mosque. This one simple question landed like a dead balloon and Naseem knew that she had hit the proverbial brick wall with the coach. It showed Naseem that her coach had little understanding of the complexity, dynamics and improbability of her having that type of conversation with a male Imam at her local mosque. She also had a sense that, as soon as she made a comment about how it was difficult for her to approach the Imam, her coach's reaction had felt like a judgement on her local mosque and that 'poor Naseem' needed rescuing from a sexist patriarchal system.

Naseem – a confident, successful professional – certainly didn't need rescuing. At this stage of coaching, she felt that it was her coach who needed support more than she did; that she could either spend time educating her coach about why her approach was falling flat or cut her losses and end the coaching. Over time she concluded that the coaching relationship was impossible and decided to end the coaching engagement.

Naseem finally found her answer working with a wonderful, empathetic and masterful executive coach. Together they agreed to have a walk and talk coaching session in a beautiful woodland park on a spring afternoon. Using nature as a metaphor for her purpose, connection and her career, both Naseem and her coach together explored what the hijab meant to Naseem. Away from the shackles of the office meeting room, the coach and the coaching had a deeper powerful impact. The coach was sensitive, intuitive and gentle. At the end of the walk Naseem decided to keep wearing her hijab.

Her final coach's skills were one of presence, compassion and curiosity about Naseem's lived experience and, as well as supporting her moving forward, the coach acknowledged her journey to this point in time. Her coach didn't push her into exploring options, come across as patronizing, judgemental or attempt to rescue her in the same way that the previous coach had.

For many clients, especially those from under-represented groups, their coaching experience would be far deeper and transformational if they had a shared identity with the coach, especially in the early to mid-stages of their career. In my personal experience, and that of many in my family, friendship group and client group, once we had flown the nest, cut the apron strings and left behind the familiarity of the education system, stepping into discovering who we were in work and life in our 20s to mid-30s felt overwhelming, confusing, isolating, stressful and emotionally exhausting.

Organizations need to offer the option of a diverse and inclusive pool of coaches so that all employees can feel that coaching is something that is applicable to them and where they feel coaches have shared lived experiences with them.

Diversity in coaching

Especially in the early years of our careers we need to have the option to **choose** to be coached by someone who we could personally connect with; a professional experienced coach with whom you don't have to explain every nuance or edit anything out. Whether this might involve social class, neuro-divergence, gender, sexuality, culture, religion or disability is dependent on the needs, goals and the choice of the coachee.

FIGURE 1.2   Rising to the top

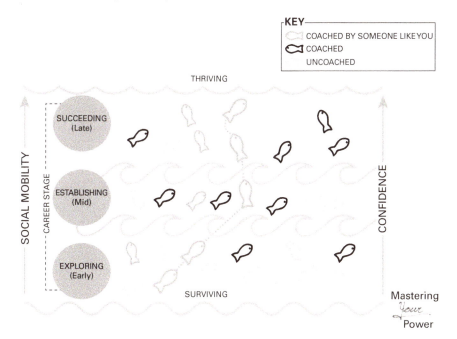

Coaching by its nature is inclusive, and any hint of elitism or conscious bias actively goes against its very ethos. However, an uncomfortable truth about today's coaching profession is the lack of diversity among professional coaches, especially in organizations and executive coaches. It is time for organizations and the profession to hold a mirror up to its own practices and explore ways of resolving systemic inertia and nested barriers.

The contradiction is that coaching is about inspiring people to maximize their personal and professional potential. However, attend any coaching conference and what you will find are the in-groups, the networks, the movers and shakers and the power brokers of the profession. What you will also observe is a distinct lack of diversity. Says one anonymous aspiring coach: 'I did a two-day taster of coaching training but just didn't feel I fitted in. Nobody looked like me or reflected my background and I decided coaching wasn't for me, so I gave up.'

I'm a strong advocate of freedom and choice and believe we need a smorgasbord of coaches to choose from. For someone from an under-represented group this is crucial, especially early on in their adult lives. In an ever-changing society, with an increasingly diverse workforce, the ability to effectively support, motivate and nurture employees is an essential target for organizations.

For a diverse workforce to flourish, organizations need coaches who understand their employees' lived experience. As employees are discovering their strengths, building confidence and getting into their stride, this can be a challenging time. It's at these moments in our lives that our imposter syndrome may be most vigorous, or people may feel they have to wear a mask to fit in and get on in work and life. Figure 1.2 is an illustration of how this is especially important during the early (exploratory) and mid (establishing) career stages.

Coaching is one of the critical tools for supporting and making a positive impact – a crucial asset in the multi-layered complexities that organizations are going to face in their new expanded role. A diverse pool of coaches is not just a nice to have, it is and will be a necessity. Regardless of which psychological theories, techniques, and frameworks are used within coaching, the coaching process relies entirely on the interpersonal interaction in one form or another. Indeed, 'the essence of coaching is putting people first' (Palmer and McDowall, 2010). Openness to support for emotional wellbeing and health varies among different populations.

Ultimately, **all** coaches need to know how to coach with a wider lens of inclusion, belonging, diversity and equity. Without these tools there is a missed opportunity; the experience for the coachee misses the mark and, as in Seema and Naseem's case, they are left feeling underwhelmed, dejected, not seen, not heard and demotivated.

Mastering Your Power Coaching framework means having the curiosity, presence, sensitivity and empathy so a client from a very different background can open up and share their lived experience. The following seven principles are the bedrock of coaching the lived experience:

- Coaching the lived experience is context based and not just content or issue based.
- Power is granted to the relationship not the coach.
- Learning is happening at an individual level and in dynamic engagement with a wider system.
- The relationship is tailored to the client.
- The coach is always steering the client towards balance, fulfilment and in the flow of their life.
- Coaching is a journey in search of patterns.
- Your attention should be on the client and not the coaching tools.

Coaching vs therapy

What both coaching and therapy have in common is that the client wants to get 'unstuck' in some area in their life to realize a fuller potential. Where therapy can help you is to learn how to heal. I would argue that a deeply transformational coaching session, where the coachee is allowed the time to think, is genuinely heard and truly seen, can also be a healing experience. Coaches are by definition not healers; yet a powerful coaching session is healing – not with the goal of healing the past but by accepting that the past is always in the present.

Generally, the coachee is looking to achieve new life goals and/or personal and professional development. The focus is on the present and the future. By integrating coaching with the lived experience and the past, this allows the coachee to relax into the present. This is not about running from the past or fighting or endorsing it. It's simply acknowledging the multi-layered lived experience. When the lived experience is acknowledged, the coachee will feel more grounded. They are able to connect with their own inner wisdom, which in itself is an empowering and revelatory process.

Coaching the lived experience focuses on the present and the coach is always steering the client towards balance, fulfilment and in the flow of their life. Therapy, on the other hand, focuses primarily on the past, where past experiences are holding someone from being fully functional and healthy. A therapist can support a client through mental health symptoms such as anxiety, depression, trauma and abuse. In coaching, the contract with the client is that they already have a strong baseline of mental health and awareness.

It is also important that as coaches we do not make assumptions about someone from an under-represented minority group.

CASE STUDY: BEATRIX

Beatrix is British-born Chinese – her parents were both born in Malaysia, of Chinese ethnicity, but came to live in the UK when they were teenagers, for school and university, and have lived here ever since. She grew up in Birmingham, UK. This is what she says:

'My first real memory of this [not belonging] was moving from primary school (I attended the local state primary) to secondary school. I guess I was quite intelligent as a child and my parents (being Chinese and traditionally quite keen on academic success) made me sit the 11-plus exam and private school entrance exams. I was lucky to be in the top six entrants for a private school in Birmingham and got a part-scholarship to attend. This reduced the yearly school fees. My parents felt compelled that I should attend as a result.

I remember going to this alien school (which needed me to travel 1.5 hours each way on two or three buses) and feeling very out of place. Very few people came from state schools, most had been in private education. Everyone felt very posh, privileged, rich. And they even seemed physically taller than me! I felt they spoke different to me (I had a mild Brummie accent; they spoke what felt to me like Queen's English...).

For many months, I used to cry regularly at home, begging my parents to send me to the local comprehensive school with my old school friends as I felt I didn't fit in there. I felt those children were from a different world to me. We weren't poor, but we weren't rich. And there were definitely some children from rich families in my class. Looking back now, everyone was really friendly and welcoming and there's nothing specific that happened that made me think about my relative status to others – but it was very much in my mind at that time. My thoughts were that I didn't want to, or need to, 'be like them' – that I was happy as I was, in the world that I had come from.

That my parents were sacrificing so much to afford my school fees never crossed my mind. It was in my first year there that this did become apparent though, and my dad ended up going to Malaysia to work as a result of a crash in the building industry and recession in the UK – we just couldn't afford our lifestyle and had very little income. He was away nearly two years, just visiting when he could. I had three younger sisters and my mum didn't work as she was looking after us all. It's crazy to think that through that time, they still paid my school fees somehow. At that point I felt even less sense of belonging at this school – my life was so different to theirs.

How did you deal with it at the time?

My first reaction was to run away – ask to be sent to another school and show my mum how sad I was about this school I was at.

In the first year of school, I sought friends, unknowingly, who were more like me and less 'like them' – those who were quieter or maybe more outcast where I felt maybe less threatened. I can't recall exactly when I felt happy to be going to that school, but naturally over time I did settle in, as I became a little more confident among my peers.

How has it impacted you in the long run?

I think one of my gremlins (negative inner critic voice) that I still have now goes back to these experiences – I have triggers around people I perceive as 'privileged' or 'entitled' and immediately distance myself from those groups – I have a tendency to box them off and make quick judgements about their viewpoints. I am super-aware when I feel more privileged than others as well – and when there are 'class' differences.

Examples would be at university, when my boyfriend (now husband) was training to be a doctor – I used to see his group of trainee doctor friends as quite privileged and perceived that they looked down on me for not doing medicine. I tended to avoid his academic social group and never really enjoyed or felt comfortable around them in social events and situations. Now I see that this was my gremlin in action.

How has this manifested itself during coaching? Eg the inner critic or gremlin.

At first, I didn't recognize that I had a gremlin on this theme; it was only through coaching that I discovered it. And even at first then, I felt it was something that was a positive thing – it protected me from being spoiled, made me feel grateful and appreciative for what I have, for example. However, through coaching, I can now see that it is also a self-defence mechanism which I can put up if I feel threatened and which could stop me from being wholly inclusive, from being empathetic and possibly from opportunities I could have to grow.

Can you share something about inclusion?

On a similar theme, I can recall quite actively distancing myself from groups of Chinese international students. I didn't want to be badged with them; I found them quite exclusive and insular as a group; they didn't integrate well with non-Chinese students. Yet they were really eager to befriend me as I was a British Chinese studying on the same course. But I wanted to associate myself with the British students, people I felt were like me. In my mind, I segregated the Chinese international students into one group and me in another. I have generally felt more 'white' than 'Chinese' as I've grown up – and often forget my ethnicity, especially in work and social situations. Looking back now, I think my assumptions were unfair and my actions probably quite unkind and selfish. That's not to say I didn't make friends with some – there were individuals I did become friendly with, but always as individuals and never as part of a large group.'

Beatrix's story is a great example of where she has a stronger loyalty and identification with her country of birth, which is Britain, and not her ancestral Malaysian Chinese family background. This dynamic may also change in the future as her parents and children get older. As her parents want to encourage Beatrix to observe Chinese family traditions, she feels the pull of two cultures and is caught up in two worlds with different expectations.

Beatrix's inner critic or gremlin is the part of her that is turned against herself, consisting of negative thoughts, beliefs and attitudes which oppose her best interests and can diminish self-esteem. In this case it was her childhood story around privilege and an aversion to those who she perceived as having a sense of entitlement. It was something she was unaware of until her coaching experience, yet this gremlin was present in her actions. It related back to a time of feeling she didn't fit in and belong at her private school, which was compounded with her family facing financial hardship.

If we applied the wider lens to Beatrix's lived experience and identity, her personal development work is around her sense of belonging, inclusion and psychological safety. During coaching our clients will not necessarily name these areas as issues. Beatrix is very articulate, intelligent and self-aware. She made the connections herself and did her own work. As masterful coaches we need to be aware that there may be more complexity around how, why and where our client is stuck or lacks confidence in a certain area.

Coaching with a systemic lens

The field of systemic coaching has gained in popularity in the evolution of the coaching profession. According to Paul Lawrence, the term 'systemic coaching', means to 'articulate the value for the coach for looking beyond the immediacy of the one-to-one coaching relationship' (2019).

We can define a human system as being a set of people in relation to one another who are organized to jointly create a particular outcome. Acknowledging and understanding the nature, impact and influence of the many different systems we belong to is one of the core philosophies underpinning the approach to this work.

A few examples of systems I belong, or have belonged to, include: family, ancestral, education, religious, work, friends, cultural, book club, gym, supper club, my child's school, political, Mastering Your Power Coaching, coaching membership body, public sector clients, private sector clients etc.

All systems' boundaries are permeable and as we seek to understand the patterns of social interaction these boundaries must be held lightly. Our different systems are nested like Russian dolls with overlapping boundaries; boundaries which can change according to what is emerging for us, our perspective and our need.

We do have a choice about belonging to some systems and can leave if they no longer serve a purpose or fulfil a need, or although we are invited, we didn't feel included: such as our membership of a coaching body, a relationship or a book club. Other systems we may have little choice over can include our education system, ancestral system or as a member of our family system.

Our clients belong to many different complex systems which are in themselves evolving, dynamic and changing shape over time. By shifting our focus to include their wider systems there is a sense of relief from our client's perspective. As coaches, we need to be receptive and engaged with how clients relate to their place in their systems. Sometimes our belonging in a particular system may present us with deeper issues, such as feeling stuck, rejected, excluded or repeating unhealthy patterns.

Coaches need to pay attention to the equity of power, psychological safety, inclusion and authenticity within these systems. As a coach, we may find ourselves exploring with our clients the notion of identity, at both the individual and collective level. While focusing on thought patterns and patterns of behaviour we need to be able to recognize that the boundaries of our systems are consistently crossing over.

When coaching we also need to be open to the hidden loyalties to certain systems, such as in Seema's case where her loyalty was far greater towards her culture and family. As coaches, we need to embrace an openness of not knowing for sure where our clients' loyalties lie, while also concurrently focusing on the patterns and interactions as they emerge during coaching.

Powerful transformational coaching is holistic and requires an awareness of systems and the interdependence of the dynamics of the different systems. Many leadership development facilitators, career and executive coaches feel they need to 'park' their client's personal and family lives (systems) outside the coaching session. By doing this they are sending out the message of excluding their clients' wider lived experience. Their reason for doing this could be a fear of a lack of skills or knowledge about dealing with personal issues. Or there might be a realistic, although unjustified, fear that they may be entering into the realms of therapy and therefore a risk to a client's wellbeing.

Any coach trained by an accredited coach training provider will be clear on the ethics around coaching and therapy. An assumption and a contract that I am making with you as a reader is that you are aware of the ethics around coaching, that you know when and how to empathetically and sensitively signpost a client towards therapy.

My observation is that as soon as the client feels understood and psychologically safe to voice their lived experience, they will talk about their different systems. This also gives them the permission to bring their whole selves to the coaching, opening the door to deeper and meaningful purposeful coaching.

Coaching from the perspective of the lived experience offers our clients the opportunity to be fully seen and heard. By learning how to do this well as coaches, through active systemic listening, our clients are less likely to leave important parts of themselves out of the coaching session.

Reflective work

The journey to coaching through the wider lens of inclusion, belonging, diversity and equity has to start with your own work as a coach. Before diving in, it is worth reflecting on these questions:

- What are your thoughts having read this chapter?
- What do you desire to do differently as a result of reading this book?
- What is your deepest intention with this work?

List ten of your closest friends (not family) who you choose to spend time with.

- How many in that list are of a different race, social class, gender, sexuality, education, income, cognitione, generation, disability to you?
- How will the findings about friends impact how you approach this work?

References

Lawrence, P (2019) What is systemic coaching? *Philosophy of Coaching: An International Journal*, 4 (2), November, 35–52

Palmer, S and McDowall, A (2010) *The Coaching Relationship, Putting People First*, Routledge, London

Shah, S (2020) Cultural differences in the coaching relationship, *Training Journal*, October, https://www.trainingjournal.com/blog/cultural-difference-coaching-relationship (archived at https://perma.cc/N6PU-CW5A)

02

Identity

Making sense of who I am

The more you know yourself, the more patience you have for what you see in others.

ERIK ERIKSON

Most of us have at some point in our lives asked ourselves the existential questions, 'Who am I?' and 'Who do I want to be?'.

In my many years of coaching experience, a client has never asked to be coached on their identity or arrived at the coaching session with the explicit goal of making sense of who they really are. Yet supporting clients to figure out the discrepancy between who they are, who they think they should be and who they really want to be is a common theme.

At the heart of the questions, questioning 'Who am I?' and 'Who do I want to be?' is a search for the core essence of who we are and our longing to reclaim our whole self. Transformational coaching is empowering and steering the client to be in the flow of their lives. Supporting them to understand and take action to close the chasm of who they truly are, and who they desire to be, is an important missing piece of the jigsaw of their lives. The power of transformational coaching is being intuitive, compassionate and curious about the emergent clues as our clients explore their identity by sharing their fears, doubts and aspirations. As coaches, we empower them with the insight to dream big.

However, significant parts of how our identity is perceived and shaped is not as fluid. This would include our relationships with significant others; our place in the systems we belong to which have shaped and influenced our sense of self; who we were as a child in our family system, our education, our role as a parent, grandparent and as a partner.

> There are also external characteristics of our identity over which we have little or no control, such as the colour of our skin, height, socio-economic class or race. This work on identity would be incomplete if we don't discuss the elephant in the room of this chapter which is the debated topic of 'privilege'. As coaches we have to also accept the impact of how privilege (or lack of) can shape and influence someone's identity. In this context **privilege is the multiple social advantages, benefits and courtesies that come with being a member of the dominant groups.**

People who are overly concerned with the impression they make, or who feel a core aspect of themselves, such as gender or sexuality, is not being expressed, can struggle acutely with their identity. This can play out in many ways such as the personality drivers behind overachievement, people-pleasing, perfectionism and being strong. Let's take a look at an example.

CASE STUDY: NABIL

Nabil, an emotionally intelligent, empathetic and masterful coach, is a gay man of British mixed-race with a Yemeni heritage. He grew up in a white family in a white neighbourhood with very little diversity. Nabil is blind in his left eye since birth. Through his own coaching work he realized he needed to explore how he had always felt about himself. A while back he noticed personal things were coming up for him in his adult life and he was curious as to where those feelings originated. The self-enquiry eventually led him to pinpoint that in his childhood there were times when he felt very different from everyone around him. He was slightly browner than all the other children. In his words he had a 'weird name' which the others would mock and make fun of. Although there was no intentional malice behind the playground teasing the experience had left Nabil with a deep-down feeling that he was different. In hindsight he realized he didn't fit in with the social groups at school, which the other children may have taken for granted.

Through his coach training Nabil had become aware of the concept of the inner critic (unhealthy internal dialogue) and accepted it was a part of our genetic makeup as human beings and the mind traps that we can fall into. His coach pinpointed that often Nabil was overly critical and overly catastrophizing. This observation led Nabil to an enquiry that there was something deeper that he needed to unpick and explore.

He reflected back to when he first started working in his organization and somebody nicknamed him 'Nibs'. He took on this persona himself and started to introduce himself as Nibs. With hindsight he realized this adoption of the nickname was a protective mechanism rooted in the potential fear of ridicule. It was a way of avoiding an awkward conversation when you say your name to people and it is met with a 'Sorry what kind of name is that?'. During these coaching conversations and self-reflection Nabil opened up to accept there was more that he needed to work on, which was also getting in his way.

In the workplace his catastrophizing was causing him to worry that he wasn't doing a good job and consequently he wasn't feeling safe in his role. Also, that he wasn't good enough to coach certain people or, when he didn't get clients, he was telling himself it was because he was different.

Looking back throughout his education his strategy for self-validation and dealing with feeling different was through high academic achievement. He had excelled and done really well at school. However, in an organization, the higher he went the less frequent became the feedback and the validation he craved. Even though he was a high performer at work, the sense of achievement and safety that came from academic results was not present.

A history of academic brilliance was now playing out as a hindrance in the workplace. His driver of being the 'perfectionist' was pushing buttons at work, as it was impossible to be perfect at everything and actually success was about being good enough.

CELEBRATING NABIL

Based on my observations of Nabil from the time we spent together, as a diverse coach from an under-represented group, Nabil has 'done the work' and in doing so his life story has given him a lot of strengths, insights and the ability to connect with people at a deeper level. He is an outstanding phenomenal coach. He has a natural instinct to know when and how to go a lot further with his clients to ensure they feel safe: a real genuine desire to connect and build rapport; to understand their map of the world to create safety. It has given him a lot of unique strengths as a coach including deep empathy and compassion.

The story of who we are is continually unfolding and evolving. With reference to Nabil's story, by connecting with who we are by acknowledging, accepting and understanding our past – by filling in the missing paragraphs, footnotes and perhaps even whole chapters, we can move forward with courage, compassion and from a place of inner strength.

Identity and life stories

Our multi-faceted identity is manifested in how we interpret our life story and how we share this narrative with others. Memories, loyalties, responsibilities, experiences, political leaning, moral attitudes, values, religious and cultural beliefs have created our sense of who we are over time. Many aspects of our identity are fluid and evolving as we mature. Our interpretation of our life stories develops and changes over time rather than staying fixed in one place.

Core to coaching through a wider systemic lens of someone from a very different background from you is the invitation to the client to:

- Share aspects of themselves through their life stories.
- Make the connections between how they see themselves and their systems.

- Take the journey to, grow, adapt and move forward.

Through powerful revealing narratives, coaches can support clients in creating deeper shifts. This approach to coaching is the opposite of pushing and prodding the client to achieve their goals with a fixed agenda.

Actively listening to life stories is a client-centric approach to coaching and requires deep presence from the coach. The skill of **noticing** what our client is presenting to us requires the coach to let go of their own personal agenda to use the tools, models and frameworks in coaching. Rogers (1959) called his approach client-centred because of the focus on the person's subjective view of the world; by accepting and acknowledging that both the coach and client are equal partners, rather than the coach as the expert. This creates a psychologically safe space for reflecting back to the coachee with compassion and directness.

As David Drake (2015) noted:

People come to coaching because at some level their old stories are not working anymore and they are searching for a new story and/or a more fitting audience for the one they want to tell. The stories that clients share in coaching conversations shed light on their efforts to reclaim, retain and/or reframe their larger narratives about who they are and who they want to be in the world. These stories generally reflect the inherent tensions between their drive for continuity (and stability) and their yearning for discontinuity (and change). At the same time, these same stories contain clues for what will resolve this tension and, thereby, lead to a new story about themselves, their lives and/or others who matter to them. It is incumbent on coaches to have the pedagogical and practical tools to work with these stories in ways that are both honouring and transformative. People generally need to name the truth before they can change it.

Systemic life stories bear the origins of our identity. During coaching, how the client describes themselves through self-narrative (including interactions with the systems they are part of) holds clues to what they want, don't want and where they are stuck. As coaches, we are listening to the words at one level, the emotions at another and how the client's self-perception, role and identity exist with their own systemic story.

Intersectionality and identity

The intersectionality framework was influenced by the work of Kimberlé Crenshaw (1989) and explored how different aspects of our identities are interwoven together such as race, gender, social class, religion, physical appearance, caste. As a theory and approach, intersectionality considers all identity markers that apply to an individual in combination, rather than considering each factor alone, and how they impact different modes of discrimination and privilege.

These overlapping social identities may be both empowering and oppressing. Consider the difference in the life experience of a middle-class South Asian female, whose parent was a diplomat, to a working-class white male from a council estate raised by a single parent. As coaches we need to be open, receptive and attentive to our power and privilege as well the power and privilege of our clients. Consequently, we can hope to avoid making a naïve assumption that we can work in a similar way regardless of their identity.

Concepts of power, privilege, oppression and intersectionality have been discussed more frequently in the public arena, especially since the 2016 election, but it is not easy to develop and apply this lens in corporations. Many diversity and inclusion initiatives unknowingly promote inclusion without the tools to integrate and support people responsibly. Thinking styles, Myers-Briggs Type Indicator, race, and gender are all seen as elements to consider, but most often separately, and with an emphasis on valuing differences. While these influences are real, and feelings, thoughts, and leadership styles matter, the expanded framework of intersectionality helps us move beyond practices that remove people from their full, cultural context.

Consider this real situation I encountered in executive coaching at a financial institution. An African-American male executive was uncomfortable navigating office relationships and was feeling like an outsider at work events. He was assigned a white, Euro-American coach who was not aware of the experience of people of colour in the corporate workplace. Her coaching strategy was to help the client construct a development plan to support him to attend more work events and feel comfortable in these social settings. The questions and challenges the coach offered misused power by dismissing the cultural context of the client as well as her own. This development plan took the executive further down the same path of disappointment, as the coach gave no acknowledgement of the structural barriers that exist. She focused more on developing his strength and endurance and the racial issue remained hidden in their coaching process.

An intersectionality approach plays out differently. I worked with an openly gay South Asian female marketing executive at an apparel corporation. She described one of the struggles in her career. Upper management had convened a group of young executives (including my client) to discuss their future career aspirations as well as the requirement of mobility. I was well into our transition coaching engagement, so a large amount of trust had already been built. She shared how her family was different than the other families being referenced in that group meeting. Rather than make the conversation about personal limitations and endurance, I acknowledged how the corporation's policies advantaged heterosexual couples. I commented on the hetero-normative relocation policies to which my client said, 'exactly', and she went on to discuss what she and her partner wanted to do long-term and, ultimately, how stressful and disheartening it was for her challenges to be made invisible in that setting. Being able to speak the unspoken and point out institutional hurdles, as well as resources and privileges the client could tap into, allowed us to develop a more authentic and empowering plan.

When Executive Coaches understand their social location (how they live in and navigate hierarchies of power, privilege and oppression, as well as those of their clients) they are better equipped to conduct themselves in an ethical manner and not replicate the micro-aggressions and oppressions that their clients experience in the world. This view is supported by research in other fields of practice. According to Rhea Almeida (2013), PhD, founder of the Institute for Family Services, 'Power is always exercised in one way or another. It is easy to intentionally or unintentionally misuse it and therefore harm others at the individual, group or institutional level.' Additionally, coaches with this lens are more qualified to work with clients to integrate solutions that include accessing privilege, power and other resources effectively and responsibly.

Deepening an understanding of intersectionality is a journey and requires an ongoing commitment to learning. Working against this development is the reality that most coaches are trained to use cultural competence and/or diversity and inclusion frameworks, and the work is stuck there.

There are, indeed, ways to expand our understanding and practice to include intersectionality. First and foremost, consider your current clients in their culture context, including their and your access to power and privilege and their and your experiences of oppression. Be open to exploring what shifts you can make in your current process, or what new coaching approaches you might employ to better connect with your clients and their objectives.

©Gail Greenstein. Used with permission. (Gail Greenstein, Institute of Coaching, Mclean, Harvard Medical School.)

Over-identification

Over-identifying is feeling someone's emotions to the point of losing our own perspective, blurring boundaries and ensuring that we cannot separate who we are from who someone else is. When we are over-identified with someone, we feel and can act as that person did.

The emotional state of over-identifying oneself to an excessive degree with someone, a role or a cause can lead to losing a sense of who we are and our identity. Over-identifying with the suffering of others we want to help, without turning towards our own emotional gaps, is counterproductive as well. We can only grow as far as the oldest parts of ourselves are integrated into the emerging new whole. Coaching is one way to explore how to move forward while reconciling the awareness of what we need to let go.

In the following sections, I'll take you through a few of the aspects of over-identification we may encounter in ourselves and in our coaching clients.

Over-identifying with our role as a parent

'I think my mother taught me what not to do. She put us first, always, sometimes to the detriment of herself. She encouraged me not to do that. She'd say being a good mother isn't all about sacrificing; it's really investing and putting yourself higher on your priority list. You can be a good mom and still work out, get your rest, have a career–or not. She encouraged me to find that balance.' (Michelle Obama, 2009)

In our role as parents, we want to support and protect our children as much as we can. It's so easy and natural to feel their pain emotionally and physically as we bandage up the cuts and bruises of grazed knees. The risk is when we start to over-parent and over-identify with our children – losing a sense of who we are. Our identity has become enmeshed in our role as a parent. 'As much as we watch to see what our children do with their lives, they are watching us to see what we do with ours. I can't tell my children to reach for the sun. All I can do is reach for it, myself.' (Joyce Maynard, writer and journalist, 2010)

An over-controlling parent will struggle to disassociate who they are and their own identity from their children's grades, income and status in life. The over-identified parent may express themselves by incessant bragging about their prodigy's every certificate, number of followers on social media or goals scored in netball or football. They may take over their children's projects and attempt to live vicariously through them.

In contrast, the over-protective smothering parent may also be the archetypal rescuer, feeling virtuous, strong, and necessary when others turn to them for help or depend on them to take care of things. The downside is that this can lead to chronic stress and a loss of their identity. A constant monitoring of how everyone else is doing leads to neglecting ourselves.

> Powerful coaching questions for the over-identifying parent:
>
> 1 Apart from your role as a parent, what are you most proud of?
> 2 Excluding your children, what is the most important thing in the world to you and why?
> 3 Do you have conversations with others that are not about your children?
> 4 Apart from your children what makes you happy?
> 5 Do your children overly worry about your happiness and emotional wellbeing?

Over-identifying with our work

Having pride and purpose in our work is a great thing, but there are certain circumstances in which this may be taken too far. '"Workism" is a belief that work is not only necessary to economic production, but also the centerpiece of one's identity and life's purpose' (Thompson, 2019). Basing our identity solely around work comes at a risk, as shown in the following example.

CASE STUDY: HARIS

I first met Haris as he was about to get promoted in his career with a major global engineering firm based out of London. All the new managers were assigned coaches and the goal of the coaching was to support him to step into his new role. Haris, in his early 40s, arrived a quarter of an hour late for our coaching session, dressed casually in crumpled chinos and an un-ironed t-shirt. Despite his appearance he came across well and was polite and pleasant; however, he was also somewhat distant and disconnected.

I was curious about Haris's mild American accent and asked more about his background. It turned out that Haris was originally from Madurai, Tamil Nadu. At the age of 24 he had got a scholarship to study in the US. He was from a fairly comfortable Muslim middle-class Indian family of business people. His family were all still in India. According to him, his move to the US was borne from wanting to experience a new way of life. Haris wasn't an economic immigrant although, when we met, I suspected he wasn't doing well financially. Haris had stayed in the US for 12 years before moving to London with his girlfriend. After a year they had split up and she had gone back to the US. By this time Haris was approaching his big 40 and was under subtle pressure from back home that he should settle down. He played with the idea of returning to the US but, as he hadn't been active about sorting out his citizenship, this was proving difficult. Nudged by friends, he turned to online dating where he met his wife and decided to stay in London.

I had a strong sense that Haris was very closed and on guard during our sessions. He would always push me to lead and was very uncomfortable answering questions which felt too personal, such as exploring his values, beliefs or future career goals. I suspected Haris didn't like to plan or talk about aspirations. In one of our coaching sessions, he arrived agitated, moody and more closed-off than usual. A presentation had gone very wrong and Haris was obviously upset. When I tried to probe further, his angry response took me by surprise, 'You can't expect me to know that. I'm an engineer. Do you realize how many years I had to study to become an engineer!'. He then mockingly told me, 'You can't expect someone like me to have to bother with this. Engineering is a very specialist career and this coaching isn't something I feel is important and take seriously. I don't know why I have to answer all these questions. I don't think you quite realize how important engineers are.' He was obviously very emotionally triggered and I suspected there was a lot more to the outburst than just a presentation going wrong. As his identity was wrapped up in his work any threat to his work provoked a highly intense response.

Once he had calmed himself down, the coaching session went back to the regular pattern of staying at a superficial level. Ultimately it was clear to me that Haris wasn't very coachable. As I reflected on what I had learnt about the experience, my conclusion was that beyond being an engineer Haris had shared very little.

Almost 15 years later our paths crossed again and Haris was still working at the same organization. He had since been promoted again and this time was dressed professionally. As we weren't coach and client, Haris was a lot more reflective and I got a better insight into his life story. He now had a 12-year-old son, was divorced and had lost his father. His main identity was still his work as an engineer, although he did mention his son – mostly in the context of which sports he was excelling at.

It turned out that many years ago, when Haris first went to the US, the culture shock had left him very anxious as he was desperate to fit in and not make a fool of himself. He had wanted to assimilate as much as possible into the American culture. What intrigued me about Haris was that he had consciously separated himself from the Indian community in the US and the UK. He was a bit of an outlier. I instinctively knew I couldn't ask too many personal details. However, as he had recently lost his dad, he was a bit more open to sharing. It became obvious that his outlier story went straight back to his childhood.

As a child he felt he didn't fit in with his family. He wasn't interested in going into the family business because he had witnessed a lot of arguments and disputes over it between his father and his brothers. He preferred the company of his friends or spending time studying engineering. His parent's marriage wasn't great. His father was emotionally and physically absent as he was consumed by running the business. His mother had many emotional issues and was also very depressed.

His maternal grandmother, who was a Christian, had eloped with his Muslim grandfather and had pretended to convert to Islam. Yet she continued secretly going to church and taking Haris with her. This was done without his father's permission. Outside the home in India Haris's friends were predominately Hindus and he felt very disconnected from his Muslim identity. The feeling of not knowing who he was or his place in the family, religion and culture had led to his over-identification with his career as an engineer. I came to the conclusion that Haris had built his entire idea of himself around his career.

Psychologists use the term 'enmeshment' to describe a situation where the boundaries between people become blurred, and individual identities lose importance. Enmeshment prevents the development of a stable, independent sense of self. In this example, Haris had become enmeshed not with another person, but with his career.

Powerful coaching questions for someone whose identity had become enmeshed with their work (Koretz, 2019):

1 How often do you think about work outside working hours?

2 Are you always thinking about work?

3 Do you have conversations with others that are not about your work?

4 Where do you spend most of your time?

5 Do your friends, colleagues or partner complain you are in the office too much?

6 Do you have hobbies outside of work that do not directly involve your work-related skills?

7 How would you feel if you could no longer continue in your profession?

8 How distressing would this be to you?

Over-identifying with feelings

Occasionally a feeling comes from nowhere and can leave us feeling overwhelmed and shaken for a prolonged period of time. I recall a meeting with a team of board directors a while ago when I mentioned that I believed it was important to consider positive action to increase diversity of coaches in the workplace. This idea was met with a deathly silence in the room. Eventually, someone spoke up disagreeing vehemently with me, citing intersectionality, and as she was a single mother, she too was diverse and didn't see why it was important for people from under-represented minority groups to get special attention. Diversity, inclusion and belonging had been on the agenda of the meeting and I was very taken back by the tone of the conversation.

With those few words I immediately felt psychologically unsafe, recalling the fear and anger I experienced in the 1980s when rumours of the National Front marching though the town centre spread fear and anger through the Asian community. I decided to walk away from working with the group on a prolonged basis. However, I was aware that I had attached more meaning and weight than was necessary to my feelings. The emotions were overwhelming. In other words, I had over-identified with the feeling to such an extent that I felt upset for many weeks afterwards and it had an impact on other unrelated aspects of work.

By working with my coach supervisor, we explored the roots of the feeling. She helped me to move on with her deep empathy, kindness and understanding, halting the feeling from taking on its own identity, stopping me in my tracks from pursuing my work and running my life.

By over-identifying with feelings, we are in danger of believing they are our permanent states and worse still they can take control and determine our destination. Feelings are just responses to certain events and people. We likely have many other feelings and experiences even when we are feeling dismissed, sad, or angry. But over-identifying with one sends them all to the background.

Powerful coaching questions for over-identifying feelings

1   What happened?

2   How did that situation make you feel?

3   How would you describe that feeling?

4   What label would you give the feeling?

5   What was it about that situation that made you feel so ...?

6   What do you want to do about it?

7   How can you move on from this?

Identity crises

An identity crisis can surface during times of change. One of the goals of coaching at the identity level is to help people incorporate practical skills and principles with which to manage life transitions and rites of passage with greater ease, flow and adaptability. When we are grounded in who we truly are, we can live deeply connected to ourselves and to others.

The process of coaching at the identity level helps people to identify their deepest fears in the form of what might be described as their 'shadow' feelings and then support them to find the resources imperative for them to reframe their relationship with these fears, opening up with the desire to live again from a deeper connection of belief and faith.

In Jhumpa Lahiri's novel *The Namesake* (2003) and its film adaptation (2007) directed by Mira Nair, Lahiri, a Bengali-American writer, draws on the immigration themes of belonging, loyalty and identity through her writing. *The Namesake* is the inner conflict of one's identity when the roots are in two very different cultures. It tells the story of a Bengali immigrant family in America, the Gangulis, and the challenges and the conflict of cultural identity experienced by different generations. Gogol Ganguli, the main character of the story, represents the portrayal of the second-generation migrant while Ashima Ganguli, the mother, stands as the representation of the first-generation migrant. Each generation deals with the different conflicts caused by cultural differences which require different ways in the effort to solve the problems (Yogita Sahni, 2014).

Cultural identity, according to Hall (1990), can always undergo some changes depending on the space and time inhabited by the individual. Hall criticizes the essential point of view that assumes that the identity is a fixed entity based on a set of characteristics that is unchanged throughout time. *The Namesake* is regarded as a novel that depicts the spirit to celebrate the transformation of cultural identity shown through the development of Gogol and Ashima who in the end adopt a flexible sense of belonging to more than one culture.

Our identity is influenced and woven into the various systems we belong to and have loyalty towards. Just as our sense of belonging, psychological safety and how we are seen and feel in a 'system' can change over time or due to events, our identity – in similar fashion – isn't steadfastly rooted and anchored in one position. Coaching with a wider lens requires an acknowledgement of the fluid and transformational nature of identity.

Tips for coaching someone from a very different background to yours

- Be prepared for a very different map of their world.
- Notice the hidden gems in their life stories.
- This kind of coaching requires greater work than just being their thought partner.
- Spend more time in the contracting and chemistry session getting to know the client.
- Be prepared that building the trust will take more time than you may be used to.
- Be curious and open about their lived experience.

- Don't assume that just because you did all of the above the client is going to share everything openly.
- Trust takes time and your client is under no obligation to share everything.
- Be open to your own biases and triggers.

Reflective work

Our identities can impact us in many ways and a deeper exploration of who we are can help us to understand those who are different from us and shape our stance as masterful coaches. These exercises will hopefully empower you on this journey.

Delving into your identity

For the purpose of this exercise, I've limited the social identity markers to just eight. I am very aware that your identity expands beyond the shortlist, but for this instance, I wanted to include aspects of our identity which are visible and therefore have a likelihood of privilege or disadvantage.

I do also recognize that our privilege and disadvantage is shaped by many other factors such as parental status, relationship status, first generation immigrant vs second generation vs third, family of origin. The list is endless so please add to the list if you feel compelled.

Table 2.1 presents eight identity markers.

Step one: Complete the Who am I column

Step two: Does this aspect of your identity give you a natural privilege or a disadvantage? Place an 'x' in the Privilege or Disadvantage column.

Step three: Add up the scores from each column.

Step four: How does your mix of privilege and disadvantage influence your stance as a coach?

What are your potential blind spots if you had to coach the person with the social identity markers in Table 2.2?

Consider the same for the person in Table 2.3.

Speak with someone whose cultural identity and background is different from yours; ask them about their family history.

With a sense of curiosity, watch a film or read a book about someone from a very different culture and identity to yours.

Afterwards, reflect on two questions: i) what did you learn from the experience? ii) What did you learn about yourself?

TABLE 2.1 Social identity: who am I?

Social Identity	Who am I	Privilege	Disadvantage
Ethnicity			
Social class			
Gender			
Sexual orientation			
Religioun			
Disability			
Neurotypical			
Age			

TABLE 2.2 Social identity: who am I?

Social Identity	Who am I	Privilege	Disadvantage
Ethnicity	Black		x
Social class	Working class		x
Gender	Female		x
Sexual orientation	LGBT+		x
Religioun	None		
Disability	No	x	
Neurotypical	Yes	x	
Age	22		x

TABLE 2.3 Social identity: who am I?

Social Identity	Who am I	Privilege	Disadvantage
Ethnicity	South Asian		x
Social class	Working class		x
Gender	Male	x	
Sexual orientation	Straight	x	

(continued)

TABLE 2.3 (*Continued*)

Social Identity	Who am I	Privilege	Disadvantage
Religioun	Muslim		x
Disability	No	x	
Neurotypical	No		x
Age	43	x	

References

Almeida, R (2013) *Cultural Equity and the Displacement of Othering,* Oxford University Press, Oxford

Crenshaw, K (1989) Demarginalizing the intersection of race and sex: A black feminist critique of antidiscrimination doctrine, feminist theory and antiracist politics, *University of Chicago Legal Forum*, Issue 1, Article 8, 139–167

Drake, D B (2015) Thrice upon a time: Narrative structure and psychology as a platform for coaching, in *The Philosophy and Practice of Coaching: Insights and Issues for a New Era* ed D B Drake, pp 51–71, Wiley, London

Greenstein, G (2018) 'Power, Privilege and Oppression: An Effective Lens for Executive Coaching', Institute of Coaching, February, instituteofcoaching.org/blogs/power-privilege-and-oppression-effective-lens-executive-coaching (archived at https://perma.cc/9QG6-VBRZ)

Hall, S (1990) Cultural identity and diaspora, in *Identity: Community, culture, difference* ed J Rutherford, pp 222–37, Lawrence & Wishart, London

Koretz, J (2019) What happens when your career becomes your whole identity, Harvard Business Review: Stress Management, hbr.org/2019/12/what-happens-when-your-career-becomes-your-whole-identity (archived at https://perma.cc/8ZN8-9J2M)

Maynard, J (2010) *At Home in the World: A Memoir,* p300, Macmillan, London

Obama, M (2009) 'Michelle Obama's tips for being happy, healthy' TODAY, October, https://www.today.com/health/michelle-obamas-tips-being-happy-healthy-1C9404528 (archived at https://perma.cc/6RHE-WF34)

Rogers, C R (1959) A theory of therapy, personality, and interpersonal relationships as developed in the client-centered framework, in *Psychology: A study of a science: Vol. 3. Formulations of the person and the social context,* ed S Koch, pp 184–256, McGraw-Hill, New York

Thompson, D (2019) Workism is making Americans miserable, The Atlantic, www.theatlantic.com/ideas/archive/2019/02/religion-workism-making-americans-miserable/583441/ (archived at https://perma.cc/44P4-2LDX)

Yogita Sahni (2014) Sense of belonging in Jhumpa Lahiri's The Namesake, *IOSR Journal of Humanities And Social Science (IOSR-JHSS)* 19 (1), Ver. XII (Feb 2014), 13–19

03

Belonging

A sense of belonging

What you seek is seeking you.

RUMI

Our sense of belonging is shaped by many interwoven layers of our lived experience, ranging from our family of origin, our ancestral map and our personal psychological biography. It can include class, the town or city where we live, caste, religion, politics – the list is endless. It is possible to add to this a story of migration, or displacement across land and sea, co-existing between languages, cultures, belief systems and traditions. Navigating these overlapping boundaries is naturally going to cause bumps in the road, misunderstandings and the need to hone strategies for survival (Shah, 2021).

Past and present feelings of not belonging can have longer term consequences as was the case with Cassie, a coach I worked with over a period of time:

> Often when I'm out of my comfort zone I can feel a dark grey cloud hanging over me. A nagging voice inside my head tells me I'm just not up to it. Over the years I've learnt to just park it to one side, bulldoze forward and just get on with it. In my teens we moved from Leicester to an inner-city London comprehensive. In my new school I felt like the odd one out country bumpkin in comparison to my slick, street-smart

classmates. I didn't feel I belonged and, on reflection, at some level this feeling has always stayed with me.

Cassie (Coach and HR Consultant)

If a move across town or a hundred miles away can have a lasting impact on feeling we don't belong, what does that mean for someone whose family, or they themselves, have emigrated across countries, continents and cultures? Or, from another angle, someone who looks visibly different from the majority group or whose accent is noticeable?

Our brains are impacted by the visual cues surrounding us. Whether it's in our family of origin, the community where you live, 'looking different' from the people around us can impact our sense of not wholly belonging. Our psyche and ego are partly influenced and reinforced when we see those around us with similar traits, so it can feel very disconcerting when you're the only person who doesn't look the same as everyone else at school or in the workplace.

A powerful depiction of this is the storyline of Randall Pearson in series five of the US show, *This is us*. Randall, a black man who has been lovingly raised in a white family, had throughout his childhood kept his sense of not belonging and inner conflict hidden from his family. In series five he joins a transracial adoption group to unpack his feelings of loss, disconnection and sadness. In this very poignant example of looking very visibly different from the rest of his family it is clear the character is on a journey to heal his wounds and untie the knots inside.

Dr Gregory Walton, Associate Professor, Department of Psychology Stanford University, developed a belonging intervention he called Attributional Retraining (Yeager and Walton, 2011). This enables people to shift from self-blame for painful experiences, such as 'I'm not good enough' or 'It's just me', to seeing that other people had experienced the same situations. The technique is brief and involves the person seeing themselves as an expert on what they have experienced and writing about that experience to help someone else.

As coaches, we need to be mindful of the complexity our clients may have with their sense of belonging. With empathy and curiosity, we must allow our clients to share their experiences and emotions behind the feeling of not belonging. We need to help them discover the tools and skills they need to thrive and not just survive. During coaching we can support our clients to see belonging as a process and not a fixed quality.

Why do we need to feel we belong?

Our need to belong is vital to our sense of wellbeing and identity. It is deeply rooted in our DNA and is observed biologically and neurologically. When this need isn't met, the impact on our psyche is devastating.

Human beings are fundamentally and inescapably motivated by a need to belong, that is, by a strong craving to form and maintain enduring mutual attachments. We are wired to seek frequent, affectively positive interactions within the context of long-term, caring relationships. There are multiple links between the need to belong and cognitive processes, emotional patterns, behavioural responses, and health and wellbeing. The desire for interpersonal attachment may well be one of the most far-reaching and integrative constructs currently available to understand human nature (Baumeister and Leary, 1995).

This deep-rooted need to belong is present from birth, and the skills associated with belonging emerge early on life as well (Over, 2016). Most of us at some point in our lives have experienced the sting of feeling excluded, left out or simply ignored. Yet our sense of belonging is complex, unique and cannot always be described in purely interpersonal terms.

Our sense of belonging is like a set of wooden Russian nested dolls. The smallest doll at the centre of the nest represents our sense of belonging to our family of origin. Unmet childhood needs, experiences of rejection, inadequacy and alienation can leave an eternal feeling of not belonging. If there is significant trauma, the coach will need to signpost the client towards therapy.

The subsequent dolls represent the various systems we belong to. The following is a sample list of some of the systems I belong to and am impacted by:

- Family;
- Culture;
- Social class;
- Religion;
- Education;
- Friends;
- Customers;
- Coaching community;
- Mastering Your Power coaches;
- Coaching bodies;
- Neighbourhood;
- Gym;
- Supper club;
- Book club.

There are many ways to be made an orphan: outright, by the parent incapable of caring for you; by the system, which demands your loyalty but trades away your uniqueness. Or by history which, through intolerance and war, has made you a refugee (Toko-pa Turner, 2017). As coaches we need to remain curious and open about our clients' sense of belonging, especially those who may have experiences of adversity in their early lives or are from an under-represented minority group.

CASE STUDY: WENDY

Wendy is a mother, wife, writer and coach in her 60s. She describes herself as white British working class. Wendy says:

'My paternal grandmother was in service from the age of eight and never went to school. My paternal grandfather was a train driver. My mother's mother was educated to the age of 12 and did factory work until she married. My mother's father was a gifted carpenter and inventor but worked as a manual labourer and struggled to make ends meet although they did own their own home. My father's family were proud council house tenants. Dad was well-educated and left school at 16 or 17. My mum had to leave school at 14, despite having a scholarship to art school, as the family needed her to go to work for the money.

Over the years, my dad rose to a senior position in a bank and my mother also worked in the same bank. They became more financially secure but never owned a home, always rented.

When I was seven we moved, from the working-class area I'd grown up in, to a middle-class suburb and I went from being the brightest kid in the school to being in the middle of the top stream and nothing special, which was a real shock. I also discovered that the way we did things at home wasn't the same way my classmates did things, and learnt to keep quiet or face ridicule about what we ate, the newspapers we read and so on. At 11, I passed an exam to go to a direct grant school. These were (so say) for the very brightest and were educational hot houses. I was a total fish out of water here among the children of academics, professors and barristers, who had learnt French and Latin, been to prep school and went abroad on holidays. It seemed like everything I knew was true about the world, from how long to cook peas to how often to wash my hair, was completely wrong. **And I internalized this as meaning there was something wrong with me.**

Throughout my life I have had many experiences which have left me feeling I didn't belong; it is something that has been with me a great deal of my life. My mother had a lot of issues and my sister was and still is very traumatized by her upbringing. My mother-in-law was very vocal with her opinion that I wasn't good enough for her son!

As a child I lied to classmates about my home life. It seemed the only option, as the truth wasn't acceptable, so I tried to make my life more like theirs in order to be accepted. It didn't work and until I was 14 or so I hung out at school with the other class misfits. In my mid-teenage years, I found that writing – something I'd always done but for myself – was a key to acceptance. I wrote a pantomime for our class to perform to raise money for the class charity and that raised my profile and status in the class and in the school. I finally had a 'thing' – something of worth that I could do and that other people noticed – and it made a huge difference. I carried on writing throughout the rest of my school career. And I made a point of being kind to people who were struggling in the same way that I had.

I'm still not completely free of it although now I recognize and name it and tend not to get hooked into it. I often recognize people who feel they don't belong and reach out to them. It made me a better parent of teenage girls – I suspect that almost all girls struggle with feelings of not belonging at some point – and I understood and took on board how painful it was when it happened to mine. (Maybe boys do too, but I have daughters.)

I didn't have the confidence to go to university, going to a teacher training college instead. All the old stuff about not fitting in came back. This manifested itself when I was being coached, as it was hard to be honest at first because of the old pattern that being honest may invite ridicule. But well worth it to deal with these very old patterns and find new ways to be.

When coaching others, I think one thing I look out for in clients is shame, because it's such an awful experience and I want to work with them to eradicate it. Often I've coached people who have had very different life experiences to me and you know what – amazingly, they all share the same problems. We all have that little voice that tells us we're not good enough. We all worry we'll be found out.

One of the things I find useful in coaching clients who are dealing with difficult people is to explore the mental image they have of that person. That's what we carry with us every day, that's the 'person' we interact with. And when we can change the mental image we have of that person, the whole perspective changes. For example, my mental image of my mother-in-law was of a huge person, towering over me. When I shrank my mental picture of her, to make her smaller than me, the whole relationship suddenly changed. I felt less frightened and more able to be in control of myself and my emotions.

At work, I never felt able to go for director-level roles. I was brilliant as a deputy but didn't have the confidence to go the extra step.

I am so grateful that, thanks to some wonderful teachers and mentors, I've learnt it's ok to be congruent and authentic and I strive to be those things as much as I can and to notice when I'm not and do better.'

CELEBRATING WENDY

I've personally known and worked with Wendy for over 30 years, before we both became coaches. She is one of the most deeply empathetic, kind and genuine people and fellow coach I have ever met. Wendy has an instinctive gift of creating safety and coaching with a depth of neutral compassion and respect. Her lived experience and the feeling of 'not belonging' has given her the unique gift of working with her clients from a deeper intuitive level. She has a radar for working with powerful personal challenges and underlying feelings of shame and inferiority that can sit with someone who has felt they don't belong.

Compensating for a lack of belonging

With our instinct for survival, we become masterful at developing the skills to fit in and survive. Yet this mastering is a false veneer of pseudo belonging. We may smile through gritted teeth or show up while hiding our loneliness and deprivation.

Many of us who have struggled with the deepest lack of belonging in our lives have also very skilfully learnt how to survive despite feeling different. In Wendy's situation she had a very successful, financially rewarding career. Throughout her working career, to compensate for the lack of belonging, she chose roles where she was an independent consultant. By staying on the fringes of the organizations and the clients she worked with she wasn't emotionally invested or part of a system where she instinctively felt she didn't belong. As a reaction to her school experience, she had throughout her working career chosen not to belong.

Wendy's strategy of boosting her self-esteem was by choosing roles where her success was measured through numerical metrics; sales targets and programming (lines of code) was her way of measuring her success which didn't involve her personal being. Similar to Nabil's story in the previous chapter, she knew that the more senior she became the fewer the people available who would have the inclination to boost her self-esteem. In her situation, it was much easier to point to numbers – on time and on budget as an IT programme manager.

Some of the common strategies that our clients may use to cope with the feelings of not belonging are shown in Table 3.1.

TABLE 3.1   Strategies to cope with feelings of not belonging

Strategy	What's happening behind the surface:
Being overly adaptable	Playing small
Too agreeable	Sense of unease
Trying too hard	Feeling psychologically unsafe
Just getting on with it without questioning it	Lack of confidence
Not rocking the boat	Feeling inferior
Politeness	Feeling insecure
Avoiding the limelight	Depression
Letting others take credit	Anxiety
Distancing from others	Fear of taking a risk
Disengaging from the work	Imposter syndrome
Not speaking up	Low self-esteem
	Low self-worth

Very often our emotional sense of not belonging may have started before we even entered the workplace. It may have started in our family of origin or our school system. Events such as social mobility and immigration can equally play havoc with our sense of belonging.

Each family has its own systemic conscience and all family members are unconsciously bound in the full dynamics of their family. By agreeing to the family dynamics, we can maintain our membership and belonging. There are family values and rules we have to follow to belong.

As a result, deciding to take our own road and do our own thing is very difficult yet can be fulfilling for many people. However, with this growth can come feelings of guilt, as demonstrated in the following example.

CASE STUDY: NITU

Nitu works as a police inspector and a career coach. She describes herself as a British Asian. She says:

'I was bought up in a strict Indian household. Although my father was fantastic and did not restrict us on clothing make up etc., we were not allowed to attend parties, or have friends over, and visit any friend's house; completely rational and accepted as the norm. I feel this was the right thing for us and kept us grounded and focused on the important aspects of life, such as education and work. Although this made me a timid shy girl which is fully expected in my culture. However, this had an impact on my work life and, going forward, on my confidence.

Speaking up was not the 'done thing'; but I was the 'black sheep' of the family and always spoke up on any injustice to me and my sister or, if anything I felt was right, I said it. I was level-headed and strong, however I was always told not to say anything because I am a girl. Having one sister and no brother made this a set up where we were brought up in a rather soft way.

I joined the police service when I was 22. Having spent my parents' money on a BSc and an MSc (oops!) I decided to ditch the degrees and apply for the police service, serving Her Majesty.

This was a massive bombshell dropped to my family; not many Asians in the service. My mum threatened to disown me if I was to take the job. My father was upset I had wasted money on degrees. My uncles were called in to explain: this is not a job for a female, who will marry you? Five years after joining the service I found my Mr Right and was married and, wow, the support I had from him and his family was so refreshing. My mother would be too embarrassed to say I took a job as a police officer but my father-in-law was phoning all his relatives and telling them proudly his daughter-in-law is in the police force.

I remember when I was being sworn in the court for becoming a police constable, all my peers were receiving various phone calls from their parents and they were so happy – I received no phone calls. In fact, my parents were very disappointed I had chosen this path.

My father said to me 'They will never promote an Asian' but four years later I had stripes on my shoulder and, a few years after that, two pips on my shoulder.

My time in the police… did I feel like I belonged? Yes, the first few years most definitely. I was at a post where there were no females and the rest were white middle-aged men, if not older. But the inclusion was definitely there. I felt energized, I felt like myself and on fire to build a career. The support was immense.

When did I ever stop belonging? The first time I stopped belonging and questioned everything was when I received a hate mail at work. I can describe this as one of the saddest moments in my career. I just felt sad, I never felt different up until that moment. But one person made me feel so low. The content of this was disturbing as I was sent some excrement with the letter.

The second time I felt I did not belong was after a number of failed promotion interviews, despite working so hard with very young children. The voices of my family were going through my head: maybe they were right, maybe I should have chosen a career that other Asian females do. The repeat failures caused me some trauma – imposter syndrome, not good enough, self-doubt, fear of failure (even now). I have reflected on why this impacted me so much; of course, it was because I was the studious one and had never failed an exam or interview ever. I wish I had some disappointments in my childhood as going through no failures meant that in my adult life I did not cope well with this.

My upbringing was fantastic but I feel it did restrict me in my career and potentially created self-doubt. The fact that females are not meant to talk in family matters, at meetings, it has been hard for me to speak up – always the quiet one, and other white colleagues are speaking what I want to say, and they are getting the credit.

I dealt with the issues by talking to others, my allies at work, my friends. **Coaching was my turning point I feel. Going through the coaching session during training, and really talking about different aspects of my life, I really felt I managed to unravel some of the issues and bring this to the surface and resolve it.'**

CELEBRATING NITU

Nitu is at the start of her journey to becoming a phenomenal coach. She is courageous and pushes herself to do the work so the best version of her shows up for her clients every time.

This story is a great example of the conflict between our loyalty and belonging in different systems. For Nitu it took a huge amount of willpower and personal strength to step away from the rules required to belong in her family of origin. Only to be let down by a racist colleague. When Nitu suffered racism at work this not surprisingly had a huge traumatic impact on her sense of belonging in a system she had trusted and, against her family's wishes, chosen to join.

Coaching someone like Nitu requires a great deal of patience, empathy and curiosity to unravel the deeper issues and feelings of rejection from her family of origin, racism at work and social conditioning which has held her back. There is also an opportunity to champion Nitu's self-awareness around courage and passion which she clearly has in abundance. A cautionary note is to remain neutral and non-judgemental about Nitu's family of origin. Although she has struggled in this relationship, she may have hidden loyalties.

Michael Fuller is a former Chief Constable of Kent police and the first ethnic minority Chief Constable in the UK. Born in 1959, his parents were of the Windrush-generation Jamaican immigrants. From a young age he grew up in care in the idyllic surroundings of Surrey. Raised lovingly by a white woman, Margaret Hurst, at 16 he joined the Metropolitan Police. His memoir, *A search for belonging*, is a poignant story of his search to belong: from his first experience of feeling he didn't belong when, at nine, a local paper described him as the 'coloured boy' in his school play, to instances of racism in the police force and then dealing with members of the black community. 'So, the thing that hurt the most was my members of my, what I saw as my own community, and they didn't see me in the same light, members of the black community in particular, calling me, and shouting about the fact that I was a traitor. And, you know, clearly there was certainly no acceptance from certain members of the black community.' (2020)

Similar to Nitu's story of coaching, there is a great deal of complexity involved in understanding and supporting someone who has experienced rejection from their cultural or family system of origin and, for example, from a work system they have chosen to belong to; especially, if they have felt excluded or rejected by their work system too. Both their stories are beautifully reflected in this extract (Powell, 2017) with a quote by bell hooks:

> She says, 'Bridges are made to walk on. So when you first become a bridge between two communities that see themselves in opposition, you will be walked on and occasionally, hopefully not too often, you will be stomped on.' But I say this, 'If the world is not bridged, if we do not have more bridges in the world, if we continue to break, we won't have a world.' So your work as bridgers, even though sometimes you'll be walked on, occasionally stomped on, is critical for the survival of a planet.

What follows is a very different story of belonging from the perspective of someone of a mixed heritage.

CASE STUDY: JANE

Jane is a coach and therapist – she describes herself as mixed heritage:

'My mother is Kenyan-Indian, with my maternal grandfather moving the family from Gujrat in Northern India to Kenya as part of the British Empire (in the 1940s). The full family then moved to the UK from Kenya in the 70s. My father is Black African, was born in Zimbabwe and grew up in Malawi; he moved to the UK in the 70s to pursue further education.

I was born and grew up in the UK in a small fishing village in south-west Wales.

Though I grew up in a community where there were no Indian or black families around for miles, it was not until I moved to London to go to university that I realized how 'different' I was and felt I didn't belong to either group.

An example of this is the societies at university: there was the Indian Society and the African-Caribbean Society – though my background meant I could join both, and I felt I could be in both societies, I also felt I belonged in neither at the same time.

Growing up close to my Indian family I was wholly accepted and loved by my aunts, uncles, grandparents and cousins and they never made me feel I was different to them in any way; however the Indian community who aren't my family are more tentative in believing that I'm Indian and are often confused when I can talk at length about religion.

My brother has an Indian name, which often confuses Indian people he meets as we all look blacker in appearance, and they often don't believe he could have any Indian heritage. An incident of this that comes to mind for me is being at my uncle's funeral and the priest telling us (me and my siblings) to stand outside the room as the ritual was only for family, as he didn't understand how we could be immediate family from our appearance.

I didn't grow up with any of my black family in the UK, which means I'm more Indian culturally/morally etc. than I am black. However, I have found the black community in the UK a lot more accepting of who I am and also a lot savvier in being able to identify I'm mixed-race without having to explain that.

The mainstream black community in the UK tends to be of Caribbean or West African (Nigerian/Ghanaian) descent, however my father is from Malawi (South East Africa) and, though there are similarities to West Africa (like there would be similarities between an Italian and a Greek person), food, rituals, traditions are quite different. As such, though I'm accepted by the mainstream black community in the UK, I don't quite fit in due to the heritage so don't quite belong. It is rare to meet a Malawian outside of Malawi and any I've met in the UK have been a distant relative/family friend so there is no tribe to connect with in the UK.

At the time the incidents didn't cause me too much upset, as any non-acceptance of who I am is a problem of the person not accepting me vs. a problem I have caused. The incidents only highlight how unaccepting groups in the world can be when you don't fit within their expectations. I've spent more time with those who do accept me to remind me that I am acceptable and loved as I am.

This series of incidents sparked the fire within me to have the curiosity to learn about others and accept them, especially when they don't fit the boxes of the normal and standard narratives as the world doesn't have the space for their identity.

It's a warming reminder to hear stories of others' experiences of 'not belonging' which manifest in many different ways but illustrate the collective commonality all humans have of experiencing a sense of not belonging.'

Jane's story of belonging is a great example of how those who don't feel they fit neatly into a box through their experience can spark the fire within themselves to be open, accepting and curious. Belonging is a very subjective experience because it is based on our personal interpretation at any point in time.

But not everyone learns how to belong. Or they lose parts of themselves, that attached them to the place where they belonged, and may feel like they're drifting aimlessly. Simply joining a group isn't enough to have that genuine feeling of belonging. We need to feel psychologically safe and accepted.

If belonging surfaces as an issue during coaching, either explicitly or implicitly, the coach needs to understand the following:

1 The need for belonging as a human experience.

2 How they can support the client to nurture and build their personal sense of belonging.

A coach needs to build their coaching toolkit to explore the automatic thoughts associated with not feeling a sense of belonging and then challenging and overcoming these thoughts to reflect on a more objective and rational grounded perspective.

Key to coaching a client to develop their sense of belonging, it is vital that they understand they are not alone in their experience, they are not 'deficient' and they are not weak. As Dr Lee Waller of Hult Ashridge Executive Education explains:

> This may help them to appropriately assign responsibility for a sense of belonging to the situation, and to maintain a more positive sense of self throughout the experience, helping them identify constructive ways to resolve it and avoid the spiral of the undermined self-concept. Coaching is a very powerful tool to support our client in understanding, identifying attributes and underlying beliefs that influence how they interpret events, which then influences how they respond to that event. Challenging these thought processes can help to make more accurate attributions, such as attributing the cause of the experience to the situation, and might help individuals to avoid the impact of a deeper sense of not belonging. (2020)

It is important that as coaches we acknowledge, show empathy and accept that our clients may be in systems where they are excluded and in circumstances where it is very difficult for them to feel they are accepted or that they do belong. Coaching our clients to identify, articulate and express the reality of what is happening in the system/situation is a pivotal stepping stone which could free them up for the deeper self-work of building their own sense of belonging. The challenge here is whether our clients feel safe enough to share how they are experiencing exclusion without feeling they won't be believed. Or, as coaches, are we sending out the message that the responsibility to feel we belong sits just on the shoulders of the client regardless of the systemic challenges?

Powerful coaching questions

1 What does 'fitting in' mean to you?

2 Where do you feel a sense of connection?

3 With whom do you feel a connection?

4 Can you name five similarities you have with 'x'?

5 What's the payoff to you for not fitting in?

6 What do you do when you feel like you belong? Why do you feel that way, and will you always feel it?

7 What if you believed that it is ok that not all our relationships will satisfy your need to belong?

8 Do you know anyone else who has felt the same?

Reflective work

There is a basic human need to belong; it satisfies things like our self-esteem and our sense of self. We are validated by the fact that we share some common ground with other people. Our belonging in each system is unconscious and we tune into what we need to do to be accepted.

We have all at some point in our lives had a feeling of not belonging – whether it's returning to work after parental leave, moving to a new school or, despite being invited to a club, having a strong sense of feeling that you just don't fit in.

- What is your personal understanding of belonging?
- Explore your own experience of not belonging to a group.
- How did you feel?
- What did you do?
- How did it impact you?
- What would you tell your 'younger' self about what happened?
- What would you do differently if you had the same experience today?
- Has it had any longer lasting implications?

A coach can unintentionally close down the coaching conversation, especially if their perspective comes from their own experience. In trying to be helpful you may actually be unhelpful. Below is a list of circumstances which may have had an adverse impact on why someone may feel they don't belong. An awareness of these issues will support all coaches in developing their active listening skills and can open up the opportunity for courageous coaching conversations.

- They are from a minority group and their social rules, values and beliefs differ from the majority group.
- Home life when growing up was very different from their school life.
- They are living in two very different cultures at home and work.
- They may have split loyalties to different systems.
- There are entanglements to their family of origin.
- They may have faced discrimination.
- They may have experienced microaggressions.

References

Baumeister, R F and Leary, M R (1995) The need to belong: Desire for interpersonal attachments as a fundamental human motivation, *Psychological Bulletin,* 117 (3), 497–529

Fogelman, D (2020) *This is us*, American TV series five, NBC network, Episodes 1–3, www.imdb.com/title/tt5555260/ (archived at perma.cc/REF7-28AP)

Fuller, M (2020) *A Search for Belonging: A story about race, identity, belonging and displacement*, Bonnier Books Ltd, London

Over, H (2016) The origins of belonging: social motivation in infants and young children, *Philosophical Transactions of The Royal Society of London Series B – Biological Sciences*, 371 (1686), doi.org/10.1098/rstb.2015.0072 (archived at perma.cc/BVN5-AMDK)

Powell, J (2017) Celebrating diversity to create an inclusive society, *Bioneers*, bioneers.org/john-powell-celebrating-diversity-create-inclusive-society-ztvz1801/ (archived at perma.cc/PK9J-99Y7)

Shah S (2021) Developing a sense of belonging through coaching, *Training Journal*, March, www.trainingjournal.com/blog/developing-sense-belonging-through-coaching (archived at perma.cc/SM76-PE7N)

Turner, Toko-pa (2017) *Belonging: Remembering Ourselves Home*, Her Own Room Press, illustrated edition

Waller, L (2020) *Sense of not belonging at work*, p37, Ashridge Hult Research Report, Hult International Business School, Berkhamsted, UK

Yeager, D and Walton, G (2011) Social-psychological interventions in education: they're not magic, *Review of Educational Research*, 81 (2), 267–301

04

Inclusion

Radical inclusion

I used to think the worst thing in life is to end up all alone. It's not. The worst thing in life is to end up with people who make you feel all alone.

ROBIN WILLIAMS, FROM THE FILM *WORLD'S GREATEST DAD*

I am going to start with the assumption that you already see yourself as an inclusive person. Someone who is well-meaning and wouldn't intentionally exclude or leave anyone out. My goal for you in reading this chapter is to support you in taking the next big leap towards becoming **radically inclusive**. Doing this isn't as easy as it may first appear. It will require facing many uncomfortable truths about the reality and impact of exclusion, bias and prejudice – especially from the lens and lived experience of those from under-represented groups.

Anyone who has endured the brutal school experience of being picked last for the netball or football team knows the gut-wrenching pang of feeling left out and excluded. Those feelings of rejection and hurt don't leave us completely and can resurface repeatedly through-out our lives. Even brief, seemingly inoffensive occurrences of rejection can sting. Eric Wesselmann and colleagues found that when participants passed a stranger who appeared to look 'through' them rather than meeting their gaze, they reported less social connection than people who made eye contact with a passing stranger (Wesselmann et al, 2012). When people are chronically rejected or excluded, however, the consequences can be more severe. 'Long-term ostracism seems to be very devastating,' say Williams and Nida (2011). 'People finally give up'.

As coaches, I strongly believe we need to embrace radical inclusion. Internally, we need to be open, non-judgemental, reflective and curious about our own personal biases, privilege and assumptions. Externally, we need to understand and have empathy with the lived experiences of those from very different backgrounds, identities, life choices, beliefs, dreams and feelings to us. Each of us has a sphere of influence around us where we can take the decision to be an ally and not just a bystander.

When I embarked on my journey of speaking up and taking action about a lack of diversity, equity and inclusion in the coaching profession, I desperately wanted to see different types of people given the opportunity to be trained up as certified professional coaches. Jill is a neurodivergent coach and a great example of why we need to increase diversity in our pool of coaches. Her personal story is an example of someone who, in spite of challenges, is today among many other roles a wonderful and incredible coach.

CASE STUDY: JILL

Jill is an internal coach and an ethics trainer for a public sector organization, who describes herself as neurodivergent, female, white and working class. She is 36 years of age, lives in London and has three children.

Jill is dyslexic and was also diagnosed as neurodivergent in her early 30s. Despite the expectation of the educational system to understand and support dyslexia, her school life was quite the opposite. Although schools at the time were becoming aware of dyslexia they were not 'inclusively aware' and her experience of the school system was intolerable. Staff still had negative associations about dyslexia and on one occasion Jill was told, 'You're stupid you will never amount to anything' by a PE teacher who had never even seen her handwriting or any of her schoolwork. The same teacher discouraged her from even thinking of furthering her education at a local sixth form.

Although at the time Jill thought it was just her written ability where she was lacking, in hindsight there were probably other things going on. Looking back, the school hadn't picked up that she had the traits of someone who was also struggling with autism and ADHD (Attention Deficit Hyperactivity Disorder). ADHD is a condition that affects people's behaviour. People with ADHD can seem restless, may have trouble concentrating and may act on impulse. As an adult, Jill finds that she has a low tolerance for frustration and if she doesn't keep things in check she can easily lose her temper.

At school, she recalls being told by teachers, 'You can't be in the club because you don't sit still – you're not disruptive but you are an inconvenience.' Jill was also severely bullied, feeling that she just didn't fit in. Not surprisingly, at the age of 15 and with no qualifications she decided to leave school and opt out of an education system which had failed her in every way.

Growing up, her home life was equally, if not more, difficult and disruptive due to her mother's severe mental health issues. Jill had been given the responsibility of raising her two younger brothers. At 11 she was asked to move into her brothers' bedroom so she could do the night feeds and nappy changes. Things only got worse at the age of 15, when her mother was admitted into a psychiatric hospital and remained there for a period of about 18 months. This left Jill with further responsibility for taking care of her siblings and running a home.

Reflecting back on this period, Jill is very aware that she was vulnerable. She had no safety net and this led to her falling in with a questionable group of people.

The pivotal positive turning point in her life was meeting her partner, with who she now has three children. As a parent Jill is determined to offer her children the safety net that she had longed for at school. She is driven to give her children the security of a home life which was missing for her while she was growing up.

In the early years of her career, she recalls a pattern. Every three years her neurodivergent traits would eventually come to the surface in whatever team she was in. She would then be moved on to a new internal department. This happened on three separate occasions for very similar reasons.

In a busy noisy office environment, due to the fact she is neurodivergent, Jill has a tendency to be very quiet and can almost disappear physically into the background. That is until she hears someone say something inappropriate. In her mind, any prejudice has crossed the line of decency and professionalism and that is unacceptable. She would then speak up bluntly and, much to her detriment, upset the casual banter and joking around in her office. This speaking up has led to her being bullied, punished and socially excluded for calling out microaggressions. Ostracized by her co-workers she would eventually be labelled as disruptive and a troublemaker. Regardless of hierarchy or position, if she hears a comment which is unethically inappropriate, Jill is very alert and empathetic to how those comments may land with others in the room. Her courage at calling out microaggressions and speaking up meant others started to name call her as the Ice Queen. If she walked into a room where everyone was chatting and relaxing, the whole group would walk out and leave. This didn't bother her at all as she was used to dealing with this kind of exclusion since her school days. Today, with experience, what she has now learnt is when, how and where it is appropriate to call out someone and give them feedback. Also, she recognizes that it's usually people who lack confidence who don't respond well to the feedback.

An incident with a very popular male colleague, who was making inappropriate sexual comments, led to him getting reported for his behaviour. Though it wasn't Jill who had reported him, Jill was ostracized, bullied and experienced a serious mental breakdown. When she returned to work after a considerable amount of time off work to heal and build her confidence, Jill decided to become a union representative herself to help others experiencing similar situations at work. She also trained to become a certified coach.

Her current role as an ethics facilitator and coach is a natural sweet spot and, at last, Jill feels she has found somewhere she fits in. She is thriving in all aspects of her work as what she does now aligns strongly with her values and purpose. She is using her coaching skills of asking powerful questions, active listening and empathy. Her role is also community facing which Jill thoroughly enjoys. Although she isn't a fan of office small talk, she will happily spend lots of time listening to those who are misunderstood. She is naturally non-judgemental and will explore the story behind their problem. Jill is deeply empathetic and compassionate.

CELEBRATING JILL

A beautiful contradiction with Jill is that although she sees herself as not being inclusive, because she doesn't fit in neatly into social groups, she is actually radically inclusive in her ability to connect deeply with microaggressions and call out inappropriate behaviour. Her coaching clients want to work with her because of her ability to ask those laser sharp insightful questions and to challenge their thinking. As a coach, she has a superpower ability to create trust and psychological safety, holding the mirror up to explore what is bubbling under the surface.

There are three key points I hope you'll extract from Jill's story:

- Jill is a powerful example of a coach who is by nature radically inclusive.
- Her lived experience of exclusion, and feeling different, gives her a deeper and unique sense of empathy and compassion as a coach. Consequently, her experiences lend themselves well to certain situations and clients.
- Note the possibilities when someone is given the opportunity to shine. That no matter what's happened in life and how much someone has been excluded and rejected there is hope. For Jill it has helped to join the dots of her life experiences, passion and purpose.

Practising radical inclusion

If you're someone who believes they are already inclusive, the following steps are an opportunity to intentionally explore this further and go deeper with this work, with the mindset to develop the skills required to coach with confidence when faced with a client who has experienced exclusion. They are in no particular order, nor is this an exhaustive list:

- What action could you take to develop a deeper understanding and empathy of the lived experience of someone who has been excluded because of their identity?
- Can you spend some time reflecting on the experience of exclusion and how this may have had an adverse impact on someone's confidence and self-belief?

- Be curious but don't rescue. If you do come across someone who has been excluded, be conscious that you're not tempted to 'rescue' as this could come across as patronizing and condescending.

- In all aspects of your work and life, consciously make an effort to include the experiences and perspectives of everyone.

- When coaching someone who has been excluded, be aware that they may have learnt to stay silent and don't assume they are quiet because they have little to say. Don't make assumptions about their experience. Instead, show empathy, stay curious and be very patient.

- Educate yourself about microaggressions (as detailed later in the chapter).

Regardless of age and life experience, we are instinctively very fast at sorting and socially self-selecting into in-groups and out-groups. It is natural and a survival strategy through social categorization to want to feel we are part of a group. Tajfel (1979) proposed that the groups which people belonged to (e.g. social class, family, football team etc.) were an important source of pride and self-esteem. Groups give us a sense of social identity: a sense of belonging to the social world. The challenge we face is our instinct to have biases towards those we consider as not being in our specific group.

Developing self-awareness around our own personal bias towards others is not straightforward. Unconscious bias is neurologically uncontrollable and scientifically undeniable. This form of bias compels each of us to divide humans into clear categories of, typically, 'same as me' (and probably safe) and 'unlike me' (and a potential risk). 'By the time we're consciously aware of the categorizations we make – young, old, female, male, Chinese, black – our brain has absorbed that information and sent it through the amygdala to the fight or flight challenge,' says Tomas Chamorro-Premuzik, a professor of business psychology at University College London and Columbia University (Rossheim, 2019). As a species, despite our brain wiring, this way is superfluous to survival in today's world.

Although there is an abundance of evidence in neuroscience of unconscious bias, we mustn't give up hope. Despite the nested systemic challenges, those of us who are motivated to change our behaviour can do so.

Understanding our own biases is an important step towards developing a radically inclusive mindset. The following are suggestions around how to do our own work in this area.

- Be curious about your own prejudices. Is there a pattern or typical scenarios where you sense you have biases?

- Before connecting with others who you suspect you're biased towards, take a moment to slow down and check in with yourself. Think of an example of when you met someone from that same group with whom you had a positive experience.

- We are more likely to be biased under pressure, so practise mindfulness and slow breathing.

- We have to learn how not to be biased; it is an ongoing learning journey.

Microaggressions

Microaggressions are a lot like acid rain. Just as acid rain can over time cause long-term damage to the eco-system of plants and organisms, buildings and statues, so subtle forms of exclusion in the form of microaggressions can impact someone's self-belief, confidence and self-worth.

A microaggression is an example of a subtle verbal or non-verbal behaviour typically targeted at someone from a marginalized group. The term was originally conceived by Harvard University psychiatrist Chester Pierce in 1970 to describe seemingly minor but damaging put-downs and indignities experienced by African-Americans.

According to Sue et al (2007), microaggressions are devastating in so many ways because they are typically ambiguous and inexplicit. Recipients of microaggressions will find themselves caught in a dilemma where there is no escape because of mutually conflicting or dependent conditions.

They may wonder whether they have been on the receiving end of prejudice or if it was all in their imagination. Because they are uncertain of whether prejudice has actually been expressed, recipients frequently find themselves in a no-win situation. If they say nothing, they risk becoming resentful and frustrated. On the other hand, speaking up could lead to the person who carried out the microaggression denying, defending or accusing the recipient of being overly sensitive or paranoid. The outcome of this is often that those on the receiving end decide to keep quiet and say nothing.

Sue (2010, 2020) describes three specific type of racial microaggressions. They are as follows:

- **Micro-assaults:** not allowing your children to date or marry outside their race, religion, caste or culture. Displaying racist marker such as swastikas.

- **Micro-insults:** verbal, nonverbal, and environmental communications that subtly convey rudeness and insensitivity that demean a person's racial heritage or identity. An example could be telling someone from an Asian background they are very articulate given their cultural background. Showing ambivalence, repeatedly forgetting or laughing when pronouncing someone's name wrong – despite being corrected.

- **Micro-invalidations:** communications that subtly exclude negate or nullify the thoughts, feelings or experiential reality. For instance, telling someone that they are being oversensitive about an inappropriate remark.

The following case study is an example of how the longer-term impact of feeling excluded and microaggressions can show up in a coaching session.

CASE STUDY: NAUREEN

Naureen is a Marketing Director, who describes herself as British Asian of Bangladeshi heritage. She says:

'At school there were a few other Bangladeshi girls in my class but I didn't have much in common with them. While their lunchtime conversations were about the latest Bollywood heartthrobs, frankly I just wasn't into that scene. I was more interested in reading Judy Blume and dreaming of being an air hostess and travelling the world. I started to notice that the Asian crowd would often meet up in each other's houses over the weekend and not invite me. My friends were mostly the white English girls and yet even with that group I wasn't invited along to the parties. Not that I could have gone anyway as I wouldn't have been allowed. My parents were very traditional and strict about me going out. I was always on the edges of conversations and gossip about what had happened outside school hours, whether this was school ski trips, discos, sporting activities or parties.

Growing up – feeling left out – was very lonely and I learnt to escape into my books, records and the radio. Being one of many in a large family it was easy to become invisible too. At 18, after a battle with my parents, I moved out of home to start university life in Southampton. It was a wonderful time – at last I'd found my tribe and I'm still in regular contact with them twenty plus years down the line. Towards the end of my university experience the bubble burst when I started applying for graduate schemes on the milk-round. The milk-round is a scheme whereby large organizations visit universities across the UK to interview and select their yearly intake of graduates. To my shock I was the only one from my whole group of friends to not have any job offers at all. It dawned on me that the world of work wasn't going be as fair and equitable as I'd imagined. The old familiarity of feeling singled out and rejected was back again.

I eventually found a job in a telecoms company and worked my way up from the support centre to bid management and eventually head of product marketing. I was hard working, conscientious, professional and very driven. On too many occasions I've had the boardroom meeting experience where the clients will address my male colleague first, even though I'm the lead account manager. If I'm with a white female colleague, she will inevitably be acknowledged before I am. For years, I tried ignoring it, brushing it off through gritted teeth, but if I'm honest it really bugs me. It hurts and although I've got used to it, at the beginning of any meeting it throws me off and I find myself second guessing myself. Or questioning if there is something wrong with me. Over the years I always felt I have had to work that bit harder to get noticed.

A few years ago, when my daughter started school, I started to get really upset if I found out she wasn't invited to a party. This was really strange because she is always a very popular child and has many invites. Although the rational and objective part of me knew she wasn't going to be invited to every single party, I was feeling hurt. On the odd occasion she wasn't invited I would be all tied up in knots, anxious and lying awake at night, plotting how I would get my own back. My daughter on the other hand has always been very nonchalant about birthday parties. The feeling of emotional pain was obviously my 'stuff' not hers and I was aware that I shouldn't project my issues on to her.

Around the same time at work, I was invited to set up the BME (Black and Minority Ethnic) network. At the beginning the senior leadership team were really positive and enthusiastic about the initiative. Much was said about how addressing race and inequality was aligned to their corporate values. My objective was to facilitate a network which was inclusive and do some ground-up work to influence a policy that made a difference through reflection and action. One of my responsibilities was also to represent the network at senior level. My approach was to work with the organization's structure and policies, share my findings and push for accountability. Very early on in the programme I recall one very hostile meeting with the senior leadership team when initially everything I said was met with a stony silence. Then, as I explained further, a few of my peers jumped in and refused to accept what I was saying. There was a flat denial of any systemic racism or need for change. I had run through my ideas beforehand with one of the team, who at the time had been very positive, but that day they were absent from the meeting. It made me wonder if they had skipped the meeting intentionally. My lone voice made me feel increasingly isolated and disconnected from my peers. I felt that, although I was superficially included, in reality this wasn't inclusion. My voice, experiences and even factual information was not heard.

The very final straw was when I realized that I had been deliberately left out of future discussions and treated like a hot potato on the issue.

I found myself completely overwhelmed and stressed out by the whole incident, so a friend suggested I started working with a coach. My coach was very experienced and highly empathetic, creating psychological safety for me to be open and honest. It felt extremely uncomfortable telling another person how I felt in case they also didn't believe me. The worst-case scenario I envisioned was if they just pretended to believe me and were really faking understanding, which she wasn't, so that was a huge relief.

My wonderful coach helped me to name what I had experienced as 'microaggression'. She also listened to my previous experiences of school and the milk-round rejection. I had never even heard the term 'microaggression' before. Previously, my view was that people just needed to toughen up and get on with it. But when it happened to me, I was incredibly upset and it took a lot of inner work to reconcile what happened. I realised that I had been so blinkered by my ambition to succeed at work that I had emotionally detached myself from the pain of feeling excluded and ignored until it was too late. It was an uncomfortable truth that I was allowed into the gang as long as I played by their rules and didn't rock the boat. I felt stuck in a system where I'm consciously and unconsciously excluded. I started noticing other colleagues who were doing the same.

Through coaching I made a lot of progress, changed jobs and now work for another organization. However, I do feel there is still much left to do.'

CELEBRATING NAUREEN

This case study is the perfect example of why we need to coach from a wider lens of systemic inclusion and equity. Initially Naureen assimilated her experiences of exclusion and rejection from school and her job search and carried on regardless. It wasn't until she started getting triggered by her daughter and then her work that she recognized that she needed to look at how feeling excluded had played a part in her life all along. Her case is reminiscent of the boiling frog parable. This is the metaphor in which if a frog is placed in boiling water, it will immediately try to save itself. However, if the frog is placed in cold water which is gradually bought to the boil it won't notice the heat until is too late. Fortunately for Naureen it wasn't too late as she found a coach where she felt safe enough to share her experience.

To study rejection with an fMRI scanner, researchers used a technique called Cyberball which Williams designed following his own experience of being suddenly excluded by two Frisbee players at the park (Williams and Jarvis, 2006). Compared with volunteers who continue to be included, those who are rejected show increased activity in the dorsal anterior cingulate and the anterior insula – two of the regions that show increased activity in response to physical pain, says Eisenberger (2012). As far as your brain is concerned, a broken heart is not so different from a broken arm.

Williams (2006) developed the three-stage need–threat model which helps to understand how people cope with ostracism and how it leads to distress:

Reflexive: at this stage the person who is excluded feels the pain and a threat to their needs for belonging, self-esteem and control. They may feel increasingly angry, distressed and sad. Little attention is paid to the context of who excluded them and why.

Coping: this phase is also described as the coping stage and this is when the person who was excluded reflects on the experience and what they do next is dependent on individual differences. Their reaction is determined by the context which can either intensify or lessen their reaction and desire to cope.

Resignation: continued exposure to exclusion can diminish the capacity to cope over a long period of time, leading to mental health issues such as feeling alienated, depression, helplessness and unworthiness.

Chen et al (2008) state that: 'Unlike physical pain, this social pain can be relived over and over again whenever the experience is recalled. This ability to relive the social pain of ostracism suggests that individuals could, after just one potent episode, continually cycle through the reflexive and coping, potentially leading to the depletion of resources that sends the individual into the resignation stage.'

Williams and Nida (2011) say: 'Although ostracism can affect all four needs, it is likely that as long as reinclusion is perceived to be possible, belonging and self-esteem needs will direct the individual to strive for reinclusion. The prospect that one can regain inclusion with someone allows the individual a sense of control over his or her future.'

Also, people who are naturally curious and actively seek out new experiences and information are better at modulating the pain of social exclusion.

Similarly, according to the social reconnection theory, if someone who is excluded is then given the opportunity to connect with others and have an opportunity to be sociable, they will do so even if there is only a remote possibility of social affiliation (for example, Maner et al, 2007; Kawamoto et al, 2015). Findings have shown that excluded individuals show a heightened willingness to make new friends. In addition, social exclusion leads to an increase in progesterone production—a hormone which is an indicator that someone is motivated to be meet others and join in with a new group (Maner et al, 2010). In conclusion, those that have experienced exclusion are still very motivated towards social acceptance – especially with those who aren't involved with their experience of social exclusion.

If we apply this model to Naureen, she had experienced exclusion previously and had moved between the two cycles of 'Reflexive' and 'Coping'. She was also very sensitive to social rejection and had finely honed skills at gaining social connections, hence her successful career trajectory. When she finally reached out to her coach it was as a result of the intensity of her desire to cope. In other words, it just got too much for her and she started to feel depleted. Also, as Naureen had a very positive university experience with friends she is still in contact with, it gives her the reserves for reinclusion.

Coaching offers a valuable opportunity to support someone who, despite having experienced exclusion, still has a desire for social contact.

Tools for coaching someone who has experienced social exclusion

- It is very important that the coach spends time building the relationship with the client to create psychological safety.
- Slow down your own cognition so you can become mindful of your own biases and distorted thinking.
- Invite the client to share their current reality so they feel heard and seen.
- Acknowledge and recognize the impact of their lived experiences.
- Patiently help the client to unpack their complex mix of emotions.
- Know how to coach and attend to strong emotions.
- Explain that it is ok to share their feelings.
- Notice when their energy shifts, check in and share you've noticed the change.
- Invite the client to name and acknowledge which of their needs have not been met.
- Ask yourself if they are in the reflexive, coping or resignation stage and be mindful of this.

- Your role is to meet your clients where they are and guide them along their journey.
- Support them to draw on their deep source of courage.
- Be patient; this isn't a time for challenging, goal-oriented coaching.

In April 2021, my marketing team ran a poll in LinkedIn with this question:

When it comes to inclusion, what do you feel is most effective in creating a work environment where people feel included?

The results were as follows:

A fair and equitable culture	48 per cent
Creating psychological safety	22 per cent
Focusing on belonging	20 per cent
Celebrating differences	10 per cent

Based on these findings, a powerful challenge for any coach is to be curious about whether their client's experiences have been fair and equitable. Interestingly, when Naureen started job hunting after university she came to the conclusion that the world of work wasn't as fair and equitable as she had expected.

Reflective work

Write down three significant times you were socially excluded:

1

2

3

- How did you feel at the time?
- How can you use your experience of social exclusion to understand others?
- Have you noticed if everyone is treated with the same respect? Perhaps there is a difference depending on gender, race, disability, sexuality, religion etc?

- Reflecting on the different systems you belong to, are some people told more about what's going on, while others are left in the dark?
- Is there a pattern as to who is left out (for example, minority women)?
- Have you ever experienced or witnessed a microaggression?
- Do you get defensive or play devil's advocate when someone is sharing their experience of exclusion?

References

Chen, Z, Williams, K D, Fitness, J and Newton, N (2008) When hurt will not heal: Exploring the capacity to relive social and physical pain, *Psychological Science,* 19 (8), 789–95

Eisenberger, N (2012) Broken hearts and broken bones: a neural perspective on the similarities between social and physical pain, *Current Directions in Psychological Science,* 21 (1), 42–47, https://sanlab.psych.ucla.edu/wp-content/uploads/sites/31/2015/05/Eisenberger2012CDPS.pdf (archived at perma.cc/9STG-7EAV)

Kawamoto, T, Ura, M and Nittono, H (2015) Intrapersonal and interpersonal processes of social exclusion, *Frontiers in Neuroscience,* 9. Doi.org/10.3389/fnins.2015.00062 (archived at perma.cc/54QA-HB68)

Maner, J, DeWall, C, Baumeister, R and Schaller, M (2007) Does social exclusion motivate interpersonal reconnection? Resolving the 'porcupine problem', *Journal of Personality and Social Psychology*, 92 (1), 42–55

Maner, J, Miller, S, Schmidt, N and Eckel, L (2010) The endocrinology of exclusion: Rejection elicits motivationally tuned changes in progesterone, *Psychological Science,* 2010, 21 (4), 581–88

Rossheim, J (2019) What neuro-science can teach us about diversity and unconscious bias, *Workhuman* blog, www.workhuman.com/resources/globoforce-blog/what-neuroscience-can-teach-us-about-diversity-and-unconscious-bias (archived at perma.cc/62XQ-8MNJ)

Sue, D W (2010) *Racial Microaggressions in Everyday Life: Race, Gender and Sexual Orientation,* John Wiley & Sons, New York

Sue, D W and Spanierman, L (2020) *Racial Microaggressions in Everyday Life: Race, Gender and Sexual Orientation,* 2nd edn, John Wiley & Sons, New York

Sue, D W et al (2007) Racial microaggressions in everyday life: Implications for clinical practice, *American Psychologist*, 62 (4), 271–86

Tajfel, H and Turner, J C (1979) An integrative theory of intergroup conflict, in *The Social Psychology of Intergroup Relations*, eds WG Austin and S Worchel, pp 33–37). Brooks/Cole, Monterey, CA

Wesselmann, E, Cardoso, F, Slater, S and Williams, K D (2012) To be looked at as though air: Civil attention matters, *Psychological Science,* 23 (2), 166–68

Williams, K D and Jarvis, B (2006) Cyberball: A program for use in research on interpersonal ostracism and acceptance, *Behavior Research Methods,* **38**, 174–180, link.springer.com/content/pdf/10.3758/BF03192765.pdf (archived at perma.cc/KDZ2-R8V2)

Williams, K D and Nida, S (2011) Ostracism: Consequences and coping, *Current Directions in Psychological Science*, 20 (2), 71–75, journals.sagepub.com/doi/abs/10.1177/0963721411402480 (archived at perma.cc/2QQ9-C8U4)

05

Entanglement

Loosening the knots of systemic entanglements

Your pain is the breaking of the shell that encloses your understanding.

KAHLIL GIBRAN, THE PROPHET (1923)

We cannot truly understand a person unless we see them as part of the rich dynamic web of connectedness to all their systems. When a client is stuck in some aspect of their lives, coaching without taking their systems into account is meaningless. Belonging to different systems simultaneously causes entanglements, inner conflict or hidden loyalties, guilt, confusion and frustration.

Picture the following scenario from the perspective of someone who considers themselves as a practising yet liberal Muslim:

1 To progress and fit in at work, as well as appear sociable, they join their colleagues in the pub at lunch time. As the consumption of alcohol is forbidden for Muslims, they choose to order a soft drink.

2 However, although they aren't drinking alcohol, internally they may still feel very uncomfortable just being in an environment where alcohol is served and is the main focus of the social interaction.

3 Added to this discomfort are overriding feelings of guilt and confusion, due to their loyalty and deeper sense of belonging to their religious system, yet simultaneously feeling conflicted over not joining in socially at work.

4 Over time, the feelings of discomfort override the desire to fit in and they start turning down the lunchtime invites.

5 Their colleagues stop asking them to join and assume they are just very unsociable.

The reality is that we all face conscious and unconscious tensions as we navigate our sense of belonging, loyalty and inclusion of many systems. Examples of systems that we are a part of might include: family, culture, religion, school, friendships, work, community etc. A new parent, returning to work after parental leave, may find themselves struggling to fit back into the system of the workplace they were in before parenthood. They may now feel out of place or, in some situations, invisible.

I have come across many parents entangled with guilt between their personal family system of parenthood vs the organizational system dynamics of conforming to long working hours. For example, they might even hide that they are leaving work early to attend a school event – pretending it's for a doctor's appointment as that would be far more acceptable in their workplace culture.

We are – in some form or other – entangled in our many systems.

The systemic coaching lens requires looking at the larger whole that someone is part of. Each of us has a constellation of systems unique to our lived and ancestral biography. We are not islands but are all connected together, through our many systems and the underlying forces that shape those systems. Incorporating a systemic lens is about understanding the mindset of a client within a larger context of the systems they belong to such as cultural, religious, socioeconomic class, organizational and educational. It's not just focusing on the immediate content of their coaching scenario or issue but looking through a wider lens.

Fitting in

In order to feel validated and complete we need to be fully seen and accepted in any system we belong to, especially our family of origin system. However, if our parents were overly dominating about who we needed to be to feel accepted and survive, this controlling and moulding will have inevitably led us to having a secret inner side – the real me vs the outer me. If the 'real me' wasn't seen or allowed, the chances are that there will be consequences later in life around our self-worth, confidence and feeling grounded.

The same thing may also be happening in the workplace where we are having to hide who we really are. Hence another layer of issues can arise about not being fully seen in those from under-represented groups when they are excluded in their organization's system.

The inner secret us and the outer us we are forced to be can lead to a psyche split – presenting ourselves differently to the world depending on the circumstances. Most of us are split in some way and feel misunderstood. Coaching and self-awareness is a powerful way of finding our way back home and anchoring ourselves. For those of us with systemic entanglements, the journey home to our true selves is not necessarily going to be straightforward and fast.

It is important to understand that a client's way of being is due to their own systemic entanglements and as coaches we must always be respectful and non-judgemental of all systems. What if there is migration in a life story? Migration, existing between languages and cultures leads to complications, losses and conflicts. The nuances of lives unfolding and settling into a host country's cultural systems should not be underestimated.

Often for those in under-represented minority groups, who may be under pressure to assimilate and conform to the majority group, the complexity of their systemic entanglements is multi-layered and the tension is greater. Assimilation is especially common when someone is an immigrant and has moved to a new country. This might even be as simple as moving from the south of England to the north of England. Over time, the accent and lifestyle may adapt but a core part of our belief systems and sense of belonging remains the same and is rooted to a part of us which feels like home.

From a systemic coaching lens, we cannot understand someone unless we truly see into and sense all their invisible dynamics and energies that they are connected to. As coaches, our lens needs to engage and look towards all their systemic forces. In Chapter 1, Seema, despite her passion for nursing, felt a greater pull towards her future husband's family system and therefore chose to leave the profession.

CASE STUDY: ELENA

Elena is a new coach, who was born in the UK and describes herself as a Chilean Brit. She is 39 years of age, married and lives in the north-east of England.

Elena's parents had arrived in the UK from Chile in 1977. Following a military coup in 1973, her father, who was a university lecturer and high up in the MIR (Revolutionary Left Movement), went underground until he was betrayed by a family member and turned over to the military. He was then incarcerated and tortured in a prison camp for almost a year. It was there that he met Elena's mother, through a relative who was also a prisoner in the same camp. During his time in prison her father decided to teach the other prisoners in the camp how to read and write. Her father has never really spoken about that time and Elena only knows what her mother has told her in recent years. On release from prison, her father was given six months to leave the country – otherwise the authorities had let him know that his life was in danger and that he would be killed. With the support of Amnesty International, he was accepted onto a university course and he moved to the UK. Her heavily pregnant mother joined him in the UK a few months later. A week after arriving in the UK, Elena's elder sister was born in a London hospital.

Her parents were only allowed back to their home country in 1990 and that was when six-year-old Elena made her first trip to Chile, where everyone assumed they were affluent and doing well. This was a complete contrast to their reality as her father now just had a low paid technician's job at a university.

The adolescent Elena was very drawn to an alternative lifestyle. At one time, she was a Goth (an offshoot of the punk genre, Goth style involves wearing dark or black clothing, dark makeup and black hair). Although her mother was accepting of this, her father was totally opposed. A very strict disciplinarian, there was a lot of pressure for her and her sister to study sciences and maths and go to university. Art was considered a 'nothing' subject. Her father was very strict about boyfriends and even as a married woman in her late 30s she has had to ask his permission if she and her husband wanted to stay over and sleep in the same room. In contrast to other children in her friendship group, her relationship with her father was one of obedience and respect. Even a flippant remark wouldn't be allowed and was verbally reprimanded.

Recently Elena's marriage has hit a crisis point as her husband – without any notice – had moved out. He had been struggling with his own mental health for many years. Just before he left, at his request, out of love to support and take care of him full-time Elena had quit her job as a team leader for a charity. Since moving out he refused to take her calls, has no fixed abode and has let her down on several occasions. Understandably, she was now struggling herself; however, she didn't want to give up on him. This wasn't the first time in their marriage this has happened. He had disappeared for long periods in the past too. She started looking for work and had been applying without any success for roles she is over-qualified for.

As much as Elena would love to have children, she felt her chances of becoming a parent were slipping away. As far as her parents were concerned, as a childless woman she had no status or voice in her family. Having children would give her this freedom as she would then be seen as worthy. Her husband had his own systemic entanglements which had undoubtedly played a part in their situation – as in any relationship, the level of interconnectedness is intensified as many different systems interlock and can cause chaos.

Divorce is frowned upon in the Chilean culture and just is not an option. During our conversation, Elena recalled a time when her parents didn't speak for a whole year yet lived in the same house and are still together. This was a light bulb moment as she recalled a previous break up with her husband, when he left and they too didn't speak for a whole year. Despite friends telling her she needs to leave her husband, Elena felt compelled to carry on. 'I know that I should be filing for divorce, I know I should, but I cannot get to that place.' She was also facing a painful decision as waiting for husband to come back to her means potentially letting go of becoming a parent herself.

CELEBRATING ELENA

Elena is a highly sensitive, caring and deeply empathetic person. Through her training as a coach, and being coached, Elena reflected back the following about herself:

- Her inner critic tells her she isn't good enough and a failure as she hasn't achieved certain things which were expected of her by her family system.

- She constantly doubts herself and her decisions, particularly if they are in opposition to her family's views and values.

- Elena has limiting beliefs about what she is capable of achieving in life.

- Her self-worth is intrinsically linked to having a family and being married and, as her marriage is failing and she is childless, this is an area of great struggle.

- Despite her growing self-awareness, Elena is still feeling very trapped and stuck.

Let's dig a bit deeper into Elena's systemic entanglements.

- Elena has a conflicting loyalty between the northern British system where she has grown up vs her family's system of origin. The rules for belonging and being seen in her family of origin system require her to be married and have children.

- To divorce in the Chilean culture is also a taboo. It isn't surprising that she is struggling with this as divorce wasn't legalized in Chile until 2004. Elena feels compelled to follow a path of staying in a very unhappy marriage. The systemic entanglement is between three systems: her family, the Chilean system and the British system. While she is childless, Elena has given up hope of ever being fully accepted by her family.

- The real Elena isn't seen completely by her family and this has caused her deeper issues of low self-worth and self-esteem.

- Her parents similarly have conflicting loyalties to Chile and the MIR (Revolutionary Left Movement) and their adopted homeland of the UK.

- For both her parents and Elena this mix of loyalties creates tension, confusion and a resistance to change.

Coaching Elena

- This isn't a goal-oriented coaching issue. The approach here is to support Elena and allow her story to be heard with neutral compassion and neutral empathy. This helps her to become aware and unravel the complexities of the different systems she belongs to and, within those systems, her hidden loyalties and tensions.

- Simply listening to the story itself won't lead to change. However, by not listening to the story we may also miss an important issue and an opportunity to explore and coach around her systemic entanglements.

- Coaching Elena on limiting beliefs and her inner critic is just meeting her halfway. By listening and being present to Elena's story there is an old injury of a lack of self-validation which is running through her life, from not being allowed to choose her subjects at school to not having a voice in her family because she hasn't had children yet.

- The art and science of exploring her 'stuckness' is looking for what is in the way. A reflective question for the coach would be: what is Elena's capacity for trust in life?

Active listening and being present

Who we are as a coach and how we show up has a huge impact in creating psychological safety and a safe space for our client to be seen and their lived experience to be heard.

Through active listening and deeply connecting with our client's many systems as coaches, we can support our clients to unpack their core issues and solve their problems at a deeper systemic level.

Masterful coaching requires us to be fully present and use our awareness focus on the complete sensory experience of being with the client. This requires not just listening to the words but also tuning intuitively into our bodies and our clients' hearts, minds, souls and the collective conscience of the wider field.

Active listening also requires the skills of identifying and revealing where our clients lack self-awareness. In Elena's case, an important breakthrough was her realization that her parent's marriage also had an episode where her father refused to speak to her mother for over a year and yet they both are still married. Impactful active listening requires listening to patterns in thought processes, choices and behaviours. A crucial skill is also practising and developing the know-how to quieten our mind. Listening deeply and giving our clients time to think is a powerful coaching tool. Coaches who have mastered this skill don't worry about asking the perfect question. Through their deep presence they intuitively know what to ask next.

R.I.S.E.N.© coaching model

The R.I.S.E.N© model is my tried and tested coaching framework, developed through coaching clients where a systemic entanglement may potentially be keeping them stuck. The model is a powerful way of loosening the tangled knot of systems and over time completely untying the knots and unclipping our wings so we can fly. Not every client is stuck because of a systemic entanglement; for some it could be a childhood story or simply a lack of self-awareness, self-esteem or fear. The model can be used in conversations, meetings and everyday leadership to unlock potential and possibilities.

R.I.S.E.N © is an acronym that stands for:

Result: identify and agree the outcome of the coaching session. Be prepared that the client may change direction during the session. If that does happen the coach will need to re-confirm they are now exploring a different result and re-contract.

Issue: identify where the client is stuck or has the challenge. It is important for the coach to be curious.

System: this stage is predominantly about listening to where and how your coachee is feeling stuck. Ask yourself is this systemic? There are three different ways a client could be stuck:

1 In the here and now: eg need to do a presentation next week and feeling nervous

2 Never-ending story with no movement: eg continual poor time management

3 Systemic – feelings entangled with our wider systems: eg a toxic work culture or a family system

Explore: discuss different scenarios, narrow down ideas and explore options for moving forward.

Nailed: coachee agrees the next steps to action.

R.I.S.E.N. provides a purpose and direction to the session by defining an outcome at the beginning, preventing it from becoming a random chat with no clear purpose. It can also be a prompt to ensure that the session stays on track. The skill of the coach is in knowing what your client needs at a particular moment, so a toolkit of different exercises and approaches is helpful to draw upon and use as appropriate.

However, a coaching session is rarely a paint by numbers exercise. Imagine a coil spring with two straight ends at the beginning and the end. At the beginning we have the 'Result' – ie agreeing and identifying what outcome the client wants from the coaching. At the other end 'Nailed' is the client's next step. This doesn't have to always be a goal or action. It could even be an acknowledgement of a new revelation or sense of self-awareness.

The emphasis is always on the coach to respond entirely to the client and their needs at a particular point in time. The important thing is to focus on the process of coaching itself – raising awareness, deepening learning, generating responsibility and building self-belief in the client.

Applying the R.I.S.E.N© model

TABLE 5.1   Applying the R.I.S.E.N.© model to Elena

Result	Elena wanted some clarity on making a decision about what to do next in her marriage
Issue	Elena's husband had moved out recently as he had been struggling with his own mental health. He left without telling her and didn't tell her where he was going. She finally managed to track him down. Despite reconnecting with him again he has continued to not show up when he has agreed to meet and hasn't returned her calls. She was distraught and deeply upset as her friends were all telling her she should divorce him. Even her parents were now saying she should leave him. However, Elena feels very stuck about divorcing him.
System	Elena is entangled with her Chilean ancestral system, her family system and the British system. On the one hand, divorce is a taboo in the Chilean system. If she remains in the marriage with the assumption of her husband coming back, she will need to face an uncomfortable truth that she may never have a child. Remaining childless means she won't be seen or be heard in her family system.
Explore	Despite her self-awareness of her own limiting beliefs and low self-worth, there was much work for her to do to figure out what she truly wanted. We did a coaching exercise of asking her the question, 'What makes you feel truly alive and your heart open up?'
Nailed	Despite the fact it was a long journey ahead with her marriage, she wanted to make it work and she acknowledged that even if it meant not having children she still wanted to be with her husband. While he sorted himself out, Elena was going to start looking for a job and focusing on her own self-worth and self-care

Coaching has typically been marketed as 'not therapy' and the focus has been on performance, tools and goals. However, clients who are emotionally and psychologically healthy may find themselves deeply stuck in some aspect of their life or triggered by a situation or a person. These clients don't always need therapy to move them forward, unless they have experienced trauma, abuse, psychological disorders, mental health or anxiety – where you should definitely refer to counselling or therapy. There are many areas where coaching systemically can be very beneficial and is empowering.

Coaching systemically doesn't require diving into the deep end of psychological trauma or shining the torch into the dark corners of the client's past systemic story. The focus is on the present and the future; however, we need to acknowledge the past and understand how systemically it has shaped the present and is impacting the future. If our deepest wish as coaches is for our clients to live their best life, experience joy, purpose and fulfilment then for some (probably many!) they will need to resolve past issues and move forward by understanding themselves better. By taking this away from coaching we are doing a disservice to our clients and the coaching profession.

If our goal is that coaching should be for everyone, then the lived experience and systemic entanglements can no longer be ignored in the coaching session.

POWERFUL SYSTEMIC QUESTIONS

Each one of us is in a permanent state of interaction with our wider field and our different systems. Everything we do or don't do has to some level an agency in our systemic story. As our personal and professional lives unfold, we may find ourselves at times frustrated, overwhelmed, conflicted and tense. Here are some powerful systemic questions which may help a stuck client:

- To whom are you being loyal when you do that?
- Who watches and smiles in agreement when you behave like that?
- Are you prepared to tolerate the guilt of doing something different?
- Who would be proud of what you're doing?
- Who are you afraid of upsetting by this decision?
- Who or what are you the most worried about now?
- What does this mean to you?
- Why do you think this happened?
- What does this remind you of?
- Who would take your side?
- What would you do differently today if you had your family's/boss's support?

- What purpose does it serve?

- Has this always been true?

- Was it ever different?

- How would an outsider explain this?

The reality is that we all face conscious and unconscious tensions as we sit in the truth of our many systems; for example, a new parent returning to work after parental leave, who may find themselves struggling to find their place and be seen again with their new identity. In some form or other we are entangled in our many systems.

The following case study is about the complexities of our place in a system when it is impacted by life events.

CASE STUDY: VICTORIA

Victoria is a financial analyst; born in the UK she describes herself as white middle-class English. She is 32 years of age and lives in Hampshire.

Victoria works for a well-known media company in one of its vertical divisions as a financial analyst. The culture where she works is highly competitive, high performance and offers high rewards. On the whole, she loves the high stakes drama. However, when we met, she was under-performing and off her game. Her boss had suggested coaching and Victoria grabbed the opportunity. Establishing what she wanted from our coaching together, Victoria made it very clear that she is focused, driven and highly ambitious, that her aim for the future is to be Chief Financial Officer and she was contemplating investing in a MBA in the future. Her initial coaching goal was to figure out if investing in an MBA was the right move.

For our first session, although Victoria was on time, she appeared slightly dishevelled and rushed. Nevertheless, she confidently shared she was aspirational and wanted to maintain – if not better – the perfect comfortable life she had already created with her husband and her growing family. I had a sense she was holding something back. Her words weren't congruent with her body language and the way she was nervously breaking eye contact. I wasn't entirely sure she believed in her own words and, as if by saying them out loud, she was convincing herself as much as telling me what she wanted.

Despite the big statements, my first impression of Victoria was that she was quite guarded and was very selective about what she shared.

Although she had initially wanted to talk about the MBA, as soon as we started exploring things, it wasn't what she really wanted to be coached on. She was just about to go off on maternity leave with her first child and was feeling quite anxious and overwhelmed about being away from work for a long period of time. She also mentioned several times that for the future she would need to earn more money to factor in care costs for her mother who had recently been diagnosed with a degenerative condition. She spoke about her mother's condition as if this was an item on her to-do list, with little emotion or concern.

We re-contracted our initial coaching session as Victoria decided she wanted to talk over how she could stay in touch with work while she was away on maternity leave, that the reality of being out of the loop at work was making her feel unusually insecure and helpless. Her inner critic was telling her she wasn't that important to the business and easily replaceable. Her organization wasn't very family friendly and I suspected Victoria herself had manoeuvred her way into her current role while her ex-boss had been on maternity leave.

I also had a feeling that her mother's condition was playing on her mind a lot more than she had shared, although she didn't seem to want to go there.

By our next session Victoria had spoken to her boss, who had been very open about jointly designing a keeping-in-touch plan. However, she was still feeling unsettled about going off on maternity leave. This time, she opened up some more and shared the pressure she was feeling about being the primary carer for her mother and her fear that her mother might have to move in with her. She described her mother as cold, dismissive, self-centred and rude. They had never been close; her visits had always been a few hours at a time and only once in a while since her father had passed away a few years ago. The thought of her mother moving in with her was emotionally suffocating and intolerable. The timing of her diagnosis had shattered her joy of becoming a mother. The only way she could handle her obligation was to pay for someone else to take care of her. A systemic question I asked was, 'Who are you afraid of upsetting with this decision?' To which, with a wry smile, she admitted that guilt was always in the background when it came to her relationship with her mother. This was now especially the case as her cousin and her husband had just moved into a much bigger house with a granny annexe as a future plan for their elderly parents.

As Victoria shared her real feelings about her mother's diagnosis, I felt a huge wave of relief in her. It was something she had been carrying around for a long time and, with her own baby on its way, the news of the diagnosis and the future uncertainty had been too much to handle. She even joked and acknowledged that life couldn't always be planned and mapped out perfectly on a spreadsheet.

Applying the R.I.S.E.N© model

Even after a powerful coaching session, where a systemic entanglement issue has been uncovered and explored, it may require more time for your client to make a major shift. We have to accept that wherever our

TABLE 5.2   Applying the R.I.S.E.N.© model to Victoria

Result	Wanted to figure out if she should do an MBA and then re-contracted to explore how to keep in touch with her work colleagues while on maternity leave.
Issue	Victoria was terrified of losing the lovely life she had created with her husband. She was very uncomfortable with the longer term uncertainty of her mother's illness and being away from work. Her deepest fear was that she would get stuck in her career and wouldn't be able to pay for her mother's care costs and she would have to take her in.
System	1. _In the here and now_. She needed to have a chat with her manager and agree how she could stay in touch while on maternity leave. 2. _Never ending story with no movement._ Ongoing work of managing her inner critic, especially when she feels she has no control 3. _Systemic._ Her place in her family system and work system was changing as she herself was going to be a mother. She had an emotional entanglement to her family especially to her mother which was triggering guilt.
Explore	We explored what was the most important thing for Victoria, which was her baby. She also realized that her own relationship with her mother was entering a new phase and she needed to explore strategies for managing this emotionally and not just practically.
Nailed	Victoria was feeling fearful about the unknown and the coaching helped her to accept what she could control and which parts she needed to let go of.

clients end up and whatever they do is the right thing for them at this junction in their lives. We have to let go of the situation just as it is and not get into an egotistical state of 'coach hero' saving the day.

Untying the knots of some systemic entanglements can take years, decades or in some cases a generation of work. Often our clients will disclose something powerful at the end of the session, knowing it is coming to an end. If this happens, acknowledge you have heard it and articulate that you appreciate them sharing this. There is something mystical, if not spiritual, in the energy between coach and client when something profound and deep is surfaced and shared: a moment of bonding and mutual respect. Often, once our clients have had their big light bulb moment, you must also be prepared for them to retrench. Remember, the work happens between the sessions, as in Victoria's case when she came back to her second session ready to open up about what was really causing her anxiety and the feeling of being overwhelmed – the systemic guilt towards her mother.

Reflective work

Write down a list of all the systems you belong to, personal and professional. For example: family, culture, social class, religion, education, friends, customers, coaching community, Mastering Your Power coaches, coaching bodies, neighbourhood, gym, supper club, book club etc.

1

2

3

4

5

6

7

8

9

10

- What is the cost and benefit of belonging to each of these individual systems?
- What is the cost and benefit of being a member of your family system?
- What is the cost and benefit of your cultural system?
- What are the hidden and not hidden rules you have to follow to belong to your family system?
- What are the hidden and not hidden rules you have to follow to belong to your cultural system?
- List all the professional work systems you have belonged to.
- Where has there been a tension between the rules you have to follow to belong to your personal system vs the rules you have to follow to belong to your organizational system?
- Which system are you the most loyal to – even though you may feel stuck and frustrated by them?
- What are you giving up in order to stay entangled within the system you are most loyal to?

Further reading

Chung, N and Demary, M (2020) *A Map is Only One Story: Twenty writers on immigration, family, and the meaning of home*, Catapult, New York

06

Trauma

What happened to you?

There is no greater agony than bearing an untold story inside you.
MAYA ANGELOU

A few years ago, I was asked to design and deliver a leadership development programme for the IT department of a very large hierarchical private sector organization. The team felt neglected, used and demotivated as they had experienced a revolving door of a long list of previous managers who had made hollow promises, not delivered and then left. Although they had lost faith in the wider organization and were initially slightly mistrusting of me and their new manager, they were surprisingly very supportive and trusting of each other. Their new Head of Digital was someone I instantly respected as he was emotionally intelligent, empathetic and visionary. He contracted to work with me as he had to deliver on highly ambitious performance targets. He also knew he had to do something radically different to motivate and inspire the team and build their psychological trust. We both agreed this would take time and wasn't a quick fix solution. I facilitated a series of leadership programmes and team coaching followed by a series of 1:1 coaching sessions for everyone. During one of my 1:1 coaching sessions, with one of the longest serving members of the team, I had one of the most powerful coaching conversations that will always stay with me.

David was in his mid-60s, just a year away from retiring, and had worked in the same organization for nearly thirty years. During the group workshops and team coaching, I had noticed he always made an extra effort to offer me cups of tea during the breaks. He came across as a gentle, kind, quiet person and a supportive member of the team. In our very first 1:1 coaching session he told me that during the previous team coaching and leadership training sessions, some of the exercises had really got him thinking and there had been several major light bulb moments. One deeply profound insight was that he now realized why throughout his life he had been terrified and too scared to speak up in meetings, to articulate his ideas and be heard. He then went on to share that his now elderly and bedridden mother had bullied him since childhood and, despite being very frail, she still continued to do so by constantly telling him he was useless, weak, ugly and that she had never wanted him. She told him that he was now and always had been a disappointment and a failure. His descriptions were so vivid that I couldn't help but picture a small vulnerable boy looking down, scared and despondent. Despite her tyranny, he was still at her beck and call, running her errands, being verbally abused, reprimanded and struggling to stick up for himself and establish his boundaries.

At the time, I was a little taken back by the depth of him opening up so vulnerably and quickly at the start our coaching session. He spoke with self-compassion, and not from a victim perspective, yet he had been subjected to a lifetime of cohesive control and rejection. What I could also sense was that he had been deeply traumatized by his mother–son relationship. He also told me that this was the first time in his life he had openly shared this with anyone and had a strong feeling that he could open up to me. My instinct was to create safety and lean into his story and not close down the strong emotions he was openly sharing, so that his lived experience could be heard and therefore he could move on. In this situation, despite a lifetime of abuse he didn't need therapy. He was emotionally resilient, fulfilled in all other aspects of his life and had a loving family of his own. For the remainder of our coaching together we spent time exploring boundaries, emotional detachment and overcoming his feelings of guilt at the thought of saying 'no' to her demands. This he successfully went on to achieve, as I received a lovely email from after his retirement wishing me well too.

David's personal circumstances had impacted how he had showed up at work and had previously stopped him from putting his views forward or contributing his ideas towards a project. As a result of our coaching work, he started to speak up earlier in team meetings, openly and assertively sharing his knowledge and experience, leading to significant savings in time and costs for mission-critical projects.

This is not the first time a coaching client has opened up about a traumatic experience and it certainly won't be the last time. Anyone who is pulled towards deep transformational coaching needs to also understand the complex dynamics of trauma. Although coaching is not therapy, it is important for coaches to recognize that trauma is often present in the coaching session and may actively be triggered and therefore require therapeutic intervention outside coaching.

According to research, about 60 to 75 per cent of individuals in North America have experienced a traumatic event at some point in their lifetime (Boyd, Lanius, Mckinnon, 2018).

Commonly experienced traumatic events can include: repeated childhood abuse, poverty, racism, bullying, physical, sexual and emotional abuse, violence, serious illness, witnessing a death, parental separation, natural disaster, serious accidents such as in a vehicle.

In coaching, we are partners with our clients in a thought-provoking and creative process to inspire them to maximize their personal and professional potential. Our clients may reach out for support in many areas of their lives. The list might include:

- Confusion to clarity;
- Fulfil potential;
- Confidence;
- Powerful decisions;

- Toxic relationships (personal and professional);
- Work–life balance;
- Time management;
- Managing stress;
- Taking risks;
- Leaving organizations;
- Leaving relationships;
- Better communication;
- Finding courage;
- Trusting themselves;
- Self-sabotage
- Reaching goals;
- Self-awareness.

It is likely that, as we support them in any or more of the above areas, a trauma story may surface. If so, we need to have the confidence, empathy and knowledge to hold this safe space.

What is trauma?

A trauma is a severe threat at some point in our life which can lead to a lasting emotional shock, preventing us from living our very best fulfilled life. Not everyone has the same reaction to a traumatic experience. The internal experience of the stressful event is like an invisible fingerprint – it varies from person to person as does the ongoing impact and survival strategy. On the other hand, just because someone has experienced a stressful event it does not necessarily mean they will develop trauma.

Different types of trauma

Acute trauma: often also described as big 'T' trauma or single incident; such as a one-off sexual or violent assault, a severe illness, natural disaster or childbirth.

Complex trauma: this is when the trauma has been repeated over a longer period of time; for example, ranging from poverty, bullying, racism, verbal and physical abuse, emotional and physical neglect, coercive control, overly strict upbringing, rejection, domestic violence to a lack of parental attachment. So David, who we met at the start of this chapter, had developed coping strategies of not speaking up and playing small to deal with a lifetime of bullying, control and verbal abuse.

Historical trauma: not only are we shaped by the genes of our parents and grandparents, there is growing research that the lived experiences of our ancestors may also impact us. Ramifications of slavery, displacement, genocide or expulsion experienced by communities and generations can subsequently result in the adoption of coping and survival strategies that are passed across generations. The impact of ancestral inter-generational trauma doesn't necessarily imply that the fear will be passed down a generation, just that we are more sensitive to it (Dias and Kessler, 2013).

Vicarious trauma: emotions can be contagious and vicarious or secondary trauma can by activated by listening to the person who experienced the trauma. This is an important area for coaches to be mindful of and where supervision in coaching is crucial. One of the consequences of deep transformational work is that we as coaches may find ourselves experiencing secondary trauma.

On 25 May 2020 the murder of African-American George Floyd by a police officer led to worldwide protests. For many people who I spoke to and coached around this time and beyond, specifically from an African-Caribbean background, there were triggers of complex and intergenerational racial trauma. Many described how they were struggling with sleeping and experiencing intense negative emotional feelings.

Perceived and actual racial discrimination has long been linked to impacting both mental and physical health. The harmful effects of discrimination include depression, psychological distress and anxiety (Williams, Neighbors and Jackson, 2003). Research (Tynes et al, 2019) has also shown that viewing distressing news directed at members of one's own racial ethnic group, or those who share the same immigration status, is related to poor mental health outcomes.

Coaching and trauma

It is not our role during coaching to diagnose trauma or attempt to heal our clients. However, we should not avoid the strong emotions which may surface if a trauma is triggered. If necessary, we should signpost our clients towards therapy. In the opening paragraphs of this chapter, David's survival strategy had, until our work together, been avoidance in dealing and speaking up to his overbearing mother. This pattern of avoidance had followed him into his work life. Through the coaching, and without any therapeutic intervention, he himself opened up and found the inner confidence to speak up and create clear boundaries with his mother.

David had experienced the complex trauma of being bullied since childhood. As a young boy he had nowhere to run to and the longevity of this situation had continued through adulthood, leaving him feeling entrapped, helpless, voiceless and overwhelmed. When we cannot escape from what is happening to us and the fight/flight strategies fail, we instead move into a state of trauma where we no longer have the energy to continue so we freeze or fragment. This leads to us dissociating from the intolerable experience and a psychological split occurs. This splitting is also described as structural dissociation (Van der Hart, Nijenhuis and Steele, 2006).

Understanding what trauma is, and how we can support our client, is important for coaches as one of the impacts of deep transformational coaching is that our intervention with clients may evoke a traumatic experience. Adapted from the work of Franz Ruppert (2014) and Julia Vaughan Smith (2019), we can say that after a traumatic event our psyche is split in three ways: the traumatized self, the survival self and the healthy self.

Traumatized self

For our clients this is the part which freezes and becomes numb during the traumatic event and from there onward will hold all emotionally distressed feelings of terror, rage, sensations, perceptions, sounds and images. It's like putting a part of themselves away into storage offsite so they can move on in their lives.

A traumatic event may have occurred when they were very young, perhaps before they even had the language or emotional capacity to understand or articulate what was happening. For example, a toddler who was left by a mother with a strict disciplinarian aunt while the mother moved overseas to find work as an economic immigrant, years later – even though the child joined their mother in the new country – the relationship is challenging, strained and feels disconnected. Later on, in adulthood, if a life event such as redundancy, divorce or relationship break-up happens, this may reactivate the trauma of being separated from their mother as a toddler. The reason for this is that the impact of the separation was never completely removed from the traumatized part and has always waited in storage. An event, a smell or an image can reactivate the trauma, leading to flashbacks, regression and feeling overwhelmed and the individual may require therapy.

WHY THIS IS IMPORTANT FOR COACHES TO UNDERSTAND

I want you to reflect on families who are separated due to migration, war or poor health. The younger the child, the more likelihood of trauma. Those from under-represented minority groups who have experienced these events may have complex histories which may surface during coaching. In some situations, the client may need signposting towards counselling or you may come across a part of them which is un-coachable. Knowing this, will give coaches the tools and confidence to serve their clients in the most appropriate way.

I recall a client whose father had died when she was three years old. Although her mother took care of the child practically, she had been emotionally detached and absent for all her childhood and adult life. The child's father was never allowed to be mentioned again. Many decades later, during our coaching together around a work issue, my client found herself emotionally overwhelmed and shaken. She also started to show signs of extreme erratic behaviour, which was out of the scope of our coaching. Until then I had always felt she was never fully emotionally present during our coaching and the work felt superficial. It was clear that a deep trauma had been triggered. This was definitely out of the scope of our coaching and we both agreed she needed counselling.

We cannot, in coaching, support our clients to integrate traumatic feelings even if they ask us for help with this. An example I experienced many years ago was a coaching client who initially contracted to work with me in the area of career coaching. During our coaching agreement I was very clear about what coaching was and we agreed the boundaries of our work together. I was confident she had understood as she came across as intelligent, 'savvy' and switched on. After a few sessions, she shared that she had been sexually abused by a family member between the ages of 10 and 16 and how her mother hadn't protected her. She revealed that she had never had any therapy and was now considering moving back to the country where her divorced mother lived – as did the person who abused her. The abuse was a hidden secret and the abuser was still living normally among the wider family. Not surprisingly, she was feeling conflicted about returning home. She told me all this very calmly and I could sense that she had a very strong survival self (see below). However, I also knew that if I continued to coach her without a therapeutic intervention there was a very high risk of reactivating her trauma and this work was outside the boundary of our coaching relationship. I listened to her situation with compassion and gently suggested that for us to continue working together she needed to explore therapy.

It is very rare to be coaching the traumatized self and these cases are the exceptions rather than the norm. As coaches we should not actively go searching for trauma; however, at the same time we need to be prepared if it does surface.

Survival self

In order to cope with any traumatic experience and survive we adopt survival skills. These can include:

- Denial;
- Avoidance of intimacy;

- Avoidance of responsibility;
- Feeling numb;
- Controlling;
- Hiding;
- Lying;
- Cheating;
- Bullying;
- Victimhood;
- Perpetrator;
- Addiction to food;
- Addiction to shopping;
- Addiction to alcohol;
- Overworking;
- Escapism through spirituality;
- Blaming others;
- Perfectionism.

These survival skills are finely honed strategies for coping and are ultimately exhausting. When we look at the survival self from the lens of those from under-represented minority groups this work becomes crucial for all coaches to grasp and understand. Picture someone raised by a traumatized parent struggling with poverty and how to make ends meet. Owing to life circumstances, the parent may have had to move country, leave their family and culture, take on several jobs and – not through any fault of their own – find themselves fully stretched and lacking the capacity to be fully emotionally available and capable of meeting their child's needs. That person may have experienced secondary trauma growing up, only to be further subjected to the complex trauma of exclusion and not fitting in at school.

Many of the case studies in this book are based on those who have had a challenging start in life and have developed powerful survival strategies. These survival strategies are how they keep themselves safe; however, in the longer term these aren't emotionally healthy strategies. Many clients with survival strategies in adulthood have used them to become high achievers, though this has usually come at a price as they often feel emotionally disconnected and struggle in many other areas of their life.

Often as coaches we hit a block with our clients. There are the clients with whom we just don't make any progress or, despite the fact that they are experiencing burnout or their personal relationships are failing, they are resisting change. In some circumstances, these clients are experts at avoiding, denying or even distracting us from coaching them fully and our time together feels transactional and hollow. We may even have a strong sense there is something they are keeping from us.

This resistance may present itself as a non-shifting limiting belief or a stubbornness about looking at the situation from a different perspective. Other examples include having fixed ideas about certain areas of their life which clients hold on to dearly. In these situations, there is a chance that we are coaching a very resistant survival self: the part our client is just not ready or willing to change or explore (yet).

As a coach we have to let go and accept that we always have to meet our client where they are. We are not there to fix and heal. Instead, we should continue to work with the parts which are the healthy self.

Healthy self

There are many ways of defining our healthy self. Personally, I like to see it as when I am at my best and feel fully alive. It's the part of me which is curious, forgiving, loving, compassionate and has empathy for myself and others, with clear boundaries and nurturing fulfilling relationships. It's being comfortable with my own company and reaching out to others for connection, experiencing all emotions fully: joy, sadness, grief, shame, disgust, anticipation, trust and excitement without becoming overwhelmed. It confers the ability to leave a relationship which is no longer working respectfully without punishing and controlling the other party, letting people get close to me with a healthy balance of trust and judgement.

It's where – through self-awareness – I find the courage to grow, express gratitude, have an abundant mindset, take risks, be curious, love and change my life.

The gift of coaching is helping our clients to explore, connect and expand their healthy self to live their best life. It involves supporting our clients on their journey to connecting with their purpose, being attuned with their true feelings so they can intentionally reach their goals.

Coaching the healthy self

In coaching we are predominantly supporting our client's personal development and, although coaching does not aim to rouse distress, we cannot ignore or discourage a client from expressing a distressing experience. Coaching has traditionally placed limited emphasis on our client's past history. However, understanding our client's background and narrative will give us valuable insight. My coaching philosophy is always to meet my clients where they are and, as part of the chemistry session, I just ask a simple question such as, 'Can you tell me a little about yourself?'. If relevant, I have also used an intake form which asks them to share a timeline of critical personal and professional compelling events. Working in corporate settings as a leadership or executive coach I'm aware that it may take time before someone is ready to share a personal story and I am mindful and sensitive about when and how to approach their life story narrative.

The crucial point in coaching is to create safety and trust for the back story to present itself and for me to be ready to coach confidently and courageously.

The following life story is a powerful example of how the survival self and the healthy self are alive and present during coaching.

CASE STUDY: KIRAN

Kiran is an internal coach, working in a senior position for a public sector organization. She describes herself as British Sikh Indian. She is 35 years old, lives in Chester, is married and has one child.

Kiran grew up in a traditional Indian family, in a council house in Salford. Her dad was born in India and her mum was born and raised in Manchester. Her parents had an arranged marriage when they were both aged around 16 or 17. Her dad left India and moved to the UK to join her mum. Kiran's eldest brother was born when her mum was 19 and her parents went on to have five more children.

During most of her childhood her parents' relationship was violent, volatile and turbulent, with many ups and downs. Her dad's lifestyle choice of excessive drinking and smoking, and his tattoos, led to him gaining the label of a 'baddy' in their wider Asian community. Early on, Kiran's mum had a sense that there was something deeper going on behind her husband's so-called 'bad' behaviour. This came to fruition as he was eventually diagnosed as a paranoid schizophrenic. At the time of diagnosis, her mum had two children and though on a good day he was loving, kind and protective and she adored him, the bad days were unbearable and she therefore tried desperately to end her marriage. Nevertheless, she was persuaded by her parents and the wider community to stay with her husband to avoid the stigma of divorce and becoming a single parent.

Due to a lack of understanding about mental health, Kiran's dad was largely disowned by the Sikh community while others took advantage of his vulnerability and used him. Kiran doesn't remember a lot about the chaos as she was quite young when things were at their worst at home. Kiran was in her late 20s when her dad died. Prior to this he had a stroke, became diabetic and used a wheelchair. In her teenage years, Kiran had also become his primary carer. Throughout our time together she spoke with great compassion, tenderness, empathy and love for her dad.

Her mum, a very strong person, raised all her six children also to be strong and financially independent. Fortunately, Kiran's grandparents were always very supportive and involved. Reflecting back, although Kiran recognized this wasn't a regular childhood, she still wouldn't change anything.

Outside the home, growing up as an Asian family in a white working-class area of Salford was emotionally tough with ongoing racism and bullying. Eventually, because of her dad's bad reputation, her family was ostracized and excluded by the wider Asian community. Similarly, there was also a feeling of being left out and excluded in her predominantly white working-class school.

In primary school and beyond, Kiran felt she was always running at a hundred miles an hour just to keep up with the other children in her class. Throughout her school years she was desperate to fit in and feel she too was 'normal' just like all her classmates. Her weekends didn't involve adventurous family days out, fun walks in parks and cosy Sunday roasts. Instead, they were physically and emotionally exhausting as the focus for Kiran and her siblings was to make sure their mum was ok by protecting her from further grief and pain while also caring for their dad. By Monday Kiran would start her school week emotionally drained and had to work extra hard just to keep up with everyone else.

My initial impression of Kiran was that she was bubbly, ambitious, earnest and full of energy. She talked fast, with great enthusiasm, and didn't leave many gaps to pause and think. It felt as if I was on an intense sprint just trying to keep up with her monologue of goals and ambitions. She also came across as highly self-motivated and self-driven. As well as her full-time career, she was studying to re-take exams to help her to get promoted to the next level. She had failed last time and it had devastated her; as far as she was concerned, this time failure wasn't an option. She had also been offered an exciting additional project to work on and had said 'yes' to that too. She confidently told me that even if it meant working a hundred hours a week, she was totally up for it. She was also trying to get pregnant and had a few projects planned while she would be on maternity leave. The focus of our coaching together was to support her in passing her exams without her becoming overwhelmed. Kiran admitted that she was very stressed most of the time, however she was adamantly resistant to change or to letting go of anything in her diary. Any exploration of finding work–life balance or prioritizing things in her life was met with a brick wall of stubborn defiance.

At the beginning of our coaching together Kiran hadn't shared in detail her childhood story. Yet intuitively I had a sense that I was coaching Kiran's survival self. She was putting herself under a huge amount of pressure, she didn't want to experience the stress she had in her life and yet was completely resistant to change. My instinct was to not challenge Kiran; instead I wanted to open up the trust and safety between us to acknowledge the contradiction between wanting and needing to change and resisting change. My coaching stance was to stay present and grounded, accepting that there was a possibility that the coaching wasn't going to have a fully transformational outcome.

Eventually she did share her back story and it was evident that there was possible childhood trauma. As she spoke with compassion, pride and non-judgement about her dad, I felt confident that at this time the likelihood of triggering the deeper trauma story was minimal. As we worked together and explored her future self, one of the main themes that filled Kiran with hope was the thought of becoming a mother herself. Although the idea of stepping away from work made her anxious, the pull towards motherhood was greater and generated powerful positive feelings.

In one coaching session, I shared the model of survival self vs healthy self. She had the realization that she had been in survival mode all her life and, even though it didn't need to be like that any more, she was still driven by her survival not healthy self.

We need to be mindful that during coaching we don't unconsciously collude with our client's survival self. When I first started working with Kiran, she wanted me to coach her 'survival self' but through patience and self-awareness the transformational work together was with her 'healthy self'. The transformational work wasn't from a place of fear of not surviving but a place of abundance, growth and freedom.

As we finished our coaching time together, I noticed that there had been a positive shift in her self-awareness. Although the initial work was exploring her purpose and future vision, the outcome was that it helped her to be in the present. Her healthy self was evolving as she started developing healthy resources. The survival self was still there; however, it was not as active and in the driving seat as in the beginning. Although she has some way to go, I am very confident that Kiran will achieve all that she wants to in her life with self-compassion by connecting and expanding her healthy self.

A trauma-informed coaching mindset

As the coaching profession is maturing and evolving, many experienced coaches are openly sharing that they have worked with traumatized clients without it crossing the boundary of therapy or counselling. I certainly have. The degree to which a coach can work with the trauma is very much dependent on your training, development and experience.

It makes sense that all coaches should develop their depth and breadth of understanding trauma and developing a trauma-informed mindset. As mentioned earlier, adverse experiences may surface during coaching. It is important that during coaching we provide safety and trust for our clients to share painful experiences and, if necessary, signpost them towards therapy. It is also important that we are at ease with our own discomfort when clients choose to share their painful experiences.

One way of supporting our clients is to coach their values and beliefs. If we apply the lens of inclusion, belonging and equity for under-represented groups we also need to ask the question whether our client's values and beliefs are their own core personal values or if they really belong to their culture, family, religion, class or caste. If they aren't their core personal values and beliefs, the further questions could be 'whose are they?' and 'is our client even aware of this?' Coaching the 'healthy self' does require developing a deeper awareness of core values. Releasing and working through secondary values to get to the core can strengthen a client immensely and instantly. This is especially significant if the trauma has displaced a person from their core values.

I have coached many clients where they have felt bullied or excluded at work in the past and now, as a reaction to this, survive by being overly competitive, critical and mistrusting. This way of thinking and behaving has become second nature and a defensive armour, regardless of the situation. In the long term, these survival strategies lead to self-sabotage, causing chaos and limiting their own success. For example, someone with a self-limiting belief that being tough and challenging is the best way to behave, may struggle to build trust and relationships with others.

I recall a client, with whom I had a very positive relationship, who recruited to the organization a new Head of Transformation, whose role was now to work with me and my team. From the outset the new Head of Transformation was closed, mistrusting, rude, dismissive and overly challenging. I found myself dreading every call and my 'survival self' started to surface. In this instance my 'survival self' was avoidance, which is what I do when I don't feel safe. I also instinctively knew that the new Head of Transformation was definitely living in fear and was also in survival mode too. Over time I discovered that this person had been ostracized and bullied in a previous organization. In this new role they were trying to make a good impression and, at the same time, were carrying a trauma they had experienced in a previous role which they had now brought into their new role.

I spent some time reflecting on the dynamic between us and decided that my 'healthy self' needed to have self-compassion. At the same time, I was curious about my own reaction. Ultimately, it was also an opportunity for me to build my own resilience and shift some of the old stories that resurfaced and were no longer serving me. Instead of being upset by what happened, I approached it as a gift as it was a reminder that we need to keep doing the work.

We need to understand that coaches also carry their own trauma which may show up through our individual 1:1 work and in the work with teams and organizations. Through self-reflection and supervision coaches have an opportunity to explore and deepen their understanding of themselves, their limiting thought patterns, self-sabotaging survival strategies, triggers and behaviours.

The work of resourcing and refreshing our healthy self is ongoing and a dynamic process of feeling connected with our true selves. Techniques for tapping into our 'healthy self' include:

- Being present and in the moment;
- Mindful breathing;
- Meditation;
- Self-compassion;
- Curiosity.

In this chapter we have explored the many different ways that a client may bring a trauma 'story' to the coaching session. Not all experiences of trauma need to be signposted and, similarly, there will be areas where coaches are not qualified to support their client's trauma. Nevertheless, if a client starts to share a traumatic story it is important to actively listen with compassion and empathy so as to avoid shutting the story down, which could exacerbate the situation for the client.

Reflective work

The following exercise is an opportunity to consciously develop your self-awareness and understand your personal survival skills. It is important to understand when we ourselves are in survival self rather than healthy self mode. This is especially essential if we are to start coaching clients who may also be in survival self mode.

- Think of a client or a situation where you felt triggered. What was the scenario? Who was there?
- How did you react in the moment?
- How did you feel afterwards?
- What did you do afterwards?
- What happened to your body physiologically when you felt triggered? For example, did your heart beat faster, or did you feel tightness in your chest? Everyone's reaction is different.
- Which emotions surface when you're triggered? Fear, anger, disappointment?
- Is there a childhood or other meaningful story surfacing when this happens?
- What support do you need, if any, to work through this?

References

Boyd, J E, Lanius, R A and McKinnon, M C (2018) Mindfulness-based treatments for posttraumatic stress disorder: a review of the treatment literature and neurobiological evidence, *Journal of Psychiatry and Neuroscience*, 43 (1), 7–25 DOI:10.1503/jpn.170021 (archived at perma.cc/E9HA-TCMY)

Dias, B G and Kessler, K J (2013) Parental olfactory experience influences behaviour and neural structure in subsequent generations, *Nature Neuroscience*, 17 (1) https://pubmed.ncbi.nlm.nih.gov/24292232/ (archived at https://perma.cc/47MT-4LPQ)

Ruppert, F (2014) *Trauma, Fear and Love*, Green Balloon Publishing, Steyning, West Sussex

Tynes, B M, Willis, H A, Stewart, A M and Hamilton, M W (2019) Race-related traumatic events online and mental health among adolescents of color, *Journal of Adolescent Health*, 65 (3), 371–377, doi.org/10.1016/j.jadohealth.2019. 03.006 (archived at perma.cc/LAK9-QK5X)

Van Der Hart, O, Nijenhuis, E R S and Steele, K (2006) *The Haunted Self: Structural Dissociation and the Treatment of Chronic Traumatization*, W W Norton & Company, New York

Vaughan Smith, J (2019) *Coaching and Trauma: From surviving to thriving*, Open University Press, Maidenhead

Williams, D R, Neighbors, H W and Jackson, J S (2003) Racial/ethnic discrimination and health: Findings from community studies, *American Journal of Public Health*, 93 (2), 200–208

07

Resilience

Redefining resilience

Do not judge me by my success, judge me by how many times I fell down and got back up again.

NELSON MANDELA, *MANDELA* DOCUMENTARY (1994)

The term 'resilience' was introduced into the English language in the early 17th century from the Latin verb **resilire**, meaning to rebound or recoil (*Concise Oxford Dictionary*, Tenth Edition).

It is the ability to adapt to stressful events and circumstances. Like the slender silver birch trees in my back garden which, despite the treacherous wintery storms, bend yet don't break.

The focus of this chapter is to explore how to coach someone from an under-represented minority group who despite their outward façade of resilience needs emotional support, empathy, inner confidence and the courage to speak up and be heard. As coaches we need to redefine our understanding of resilience from the lens of someone from a minority group. Resilience is a complex dynamic, with many multiple layers, specifically from the perspective of someone who has had no choice but to stay strong to survive.

My life has definitely had its very fair share of twist and turns. Sometimes it has felt as if I'm setting out for a gentle sail on a beautiful sunny summer afternoon only to discover that with one turn I am white water rafting! More than once unexpected events have thrown me a character-building curveball. In reality, for many years this ability to keep going, regardless of the circumstances, came at a very heavy price. This resilience was from my 'survival self' and not my 'healthy self' as explored in Chapter 6.

Ever since I can remember I've been an avid reader of personal development and growth books. In my teens, it was through fiction and trying to understand myself in the context of the world outside my home life. Books like Judy Blume's *Are you there God? It's me Margaret* or J D Salinger's *Franny and Zooey* plus many more. As I got older, my reading had a wider arc: from social anthropology, neuroscience and brain wiring all the way to the Toltec wisdom of *The Four Agreements* by the shamanic healer and teacher Don Miguel Ruiz to the poetry of Khalil Gibran – plus everything in between. On reflection, the one area of personal development books that I haven't actively sought out have been non-fiction books about how to develop my inner strength, grit or how to be more resilient. I didn't need to read a book to learn how to be strong and resilient. Being tough, adaptable, bouncing back and carrying on regardless was a learnt behaviour and a core survival strategy.

In reality, my resilient self was like a fragile pyramid of playing cards: pull the wrong card and everything could come crashing down.

Growing up, I was taught the values of patience, hard work, intuition and wisdom; also, that every action always has a consequence. My parents were hardworking immigrants; they both kept their heads down, worked seven days a week, faced racism, prejudice and, in my mum's case, also battled sexism from the Asian community. They were both separated from their own parents, in a foreign country and a new home which was at times very unwelcoming and hostile. Yet they carried on day after day, week after week, decade after decade. It was all about survival and building security for their children, making sure we got a good education and a better life than theirs. I too was learning to keep my head down, make sacrifices, keep going and be strong. In my 30s, just before I trained as a coach, my life was very similar to theirs. The only difference was social mobility and the lifestyle trappings of the occasional holiday or treat.

What I needed was to learn how to be better at having my voice heard, reaching out for help and asking for my needs to be met: to allow myself to be vulnerable yet at the same time feel psychologically safe. Being strong, but without having your needs met and not being in touch with your emotions, is in the long run just existing and not living life to the full. It is a bit like peering through from the outside while everyone else is enjoying the party inside.

Maria's case study is a powerful and complex scenario of someone who initially comes across as resilient and strong. However, behind this resilience are layers of vulnerability and systemic challenges due to her family of origin and culture, through to racism and prejudice at work.

CASE STUDY: MARIA

Maria describes herself as Black African; she is in her late 30s and was born in Portugal to parents from Cape Verde. She has lived in Hertfordshire in the UK for the last 18 years. Maria works in marketing for a private sector organization. She is also a coach and mentor.

About 50 years ago, when her parents were in their mid-20s, they moved to Portugal from Cape Verde, East Africa. Maria was born in Portugal and is the youngest of five siblings. Her father built their family home in Portugal in an area which in Maria's words, 'some would describe as a ghetto'. It was where she lived until the age of 11, in a large community of African immigrant neighbours and mainly friends and family from Cape Verde.

Maria grew up surrounded by family and a large supportive community which kept an eye out for each other's children and overall wellbeing. Even though she went to the local Portuguese school, her home life back in the ghetto was similar to the life and culture one would expect in Cape Verde. The weekends were packed with people coming together sharing food, partying and socializing. Her parents experienced many incidents of overt racism when they first moved to Portugal and things on that front didn't change too much as Maria grew up. She describes her parents as hard working, good citizens who diligently followed the rules. These are values which have been passed on to Maria and all her siblings too.

When Maria was 11, her parents' turbulent marriage came to end as her mother – with the support of her older children – moved out and bought a house in a white area. Typical of her proud mother, she refused to ask for help and they would often have no food for several days on end. Not asking for help is a behaviour pattern that Maria has discovered she too had learnt to copy until recently. Her parents' divorce itself was very traumatic as her dad was opposed to the marriage ending. After the divorce Maria's father refused to speak to the older siblings as he felt betrayed by them. Culturally, divorce was a taboo, even if the marriage was very dysfunctional and abusive. Women weren't supposed to leave husbands and were ostracized and punished by the wider community for doing so. Maria describes her mum's decision to leave as 'pioneering and hugely courageous'. She says:

'I don't remember my parents having a healthy relationship. In fact, I don't remember them even talking to one another. There was always tension at home and, when they were both in the same room, I remember being afraid that the smallest incident would start an argument. There is a particular episode that always comes to mind when I think now about my parents' relationship. I must have been eight or nine, and I have this vivid memory of my dad raising his hand to hit my mum. At that young age, my sister and I jumped in between to prevent it from happening and it's something I'll never be able to forget. I don't remember sleeping on my own when I was living with my parents because my mum would come and sleep in my bed. She did that to protect herself from violence. There was always tension and anxiety in case someone said the wrong thing that could trigger another violent episode.

After 21 years of marriage, my mum decided to ask for a divorce and she went on to raise five children on her own. For many years after that, I used to say I didn't want to get married because it always ends up in divorce. I'm glad to say that I have a different perspective nowadays.

My way of dealing with it was to shut down and become 'invisible'. By doing so, I knew it was the best way of keeping myself away from trouble. As an adult, I've struggled to speak up in different occasions, especially at work. It's taken years for me to understand exactly why I shut down. It turns out I've used being quiet as a coping mechanism to keep me safe when my father was being violent or when there was an argument at home. However, as an adult that reflects in me taking my time to speak up or not doing so at all.

I've always known that unlike my siblings I didn't want to end up working in a store. I wanted to do something different and meaningful. I enrolled to study sociology at university for four years. After this I decided to move to the UK and then Malta, where I also faced quite a bit of racism. I moved from the UK to work for a company where they would arrange accommodation for the first month. On my very first day the owner who had hired me hadn't known that I was black until I arrived. He took me aside and sensitively let me know that I should be aware that there was some racism and I needed to be careful. Also, that when I was walking around, people might look at me strangely. My initial thoughts were full of trepidation and worry about what I had walked into. Watching what happened to my mum toughened me up.'

I was curious about how Maria's back story had manifested itself during coaching and being coached. She told me, 'It's reflected in both, I believe. When I'm coaching someone, I struggle at times to ask the so-called 'difficult questions' because I don't want to make someone feel uncomfortable. I don't want them to shut down as I sometimes do when someone says or does something that can be triggering.'

CELEBRATING MARIA

Maria is the embodiment of a coach who is working on herself. Initially, she became a very capable transactional coach who is very skilled at intentionally using all the coaching competencies and linear coaching models of powerful questions, active listening and contracting. Her natural compassion and integrity enable her to create psychological safety and client trust. However, as she recognized that she herself needed therapy, this extra level of self-awareness has made her grow into a powerful transformational coach. The more she is opening up and getting in touch with how her back story has been playing out and impacting her, the more impactful her client work.

Maria has also been working with a range of clients, including those from under-represented minority groups. Due to her self-awareness, supervision and integrity Maria is able to avoid colluding or projecting her own story. Instead, she can sensitively lean in with empathy, courage and kindness. Her clients are professionals from diverse and similar ethnic backgrounds. They feel safe enough to open up quickly, without feeling misunderstood or judged. They don't edit things out, concerned that it will take too long to explain their background, and at the same time they don't waste time with lengthy explanations of the multi-layered complexities. Maria is able to ask powerful questions without the fear of triggering herself or her clients.

When I first met Maria, she came across as someone who was highly compassionate, had integrity, yet was emotionally reserved and at the same time very resilient. There were many contradictions in her. She wanted to connect and open up, however, at the same time she was clearly keeping everyone at arm's length. I had a feeling that I had to be patient and take time creating trust between us. She was good at thinking things through and making sound rational decisions, however, if you asked her to open up and explore emotional needs or get in touch with her true feelings then the barriers would come down. While we were working together, there was a new romantic partner on the horizon and this had thrown her into emotional turmoil.

During a powerful 'values' exercise together we explored the life story narrative behind her values. Once she had listed these values and reflected on where she had obtained them we then went back to the list again. This time we looked at them from the systemic lens of those which were truly her 'values' and those she needed to let go of as they belonged to her family, culture or other systems and were no longer serving her. Later, Maria told me that this one exercise was pivotal in moving her forward. It's an exercise she has used with her clients too.

Our work together also made her realize that she needed to have therapy to understand why she closes up and shuts down. Although coaching opened the door to self-exploration and taking the steps towards a fulfilling future life, it also brought to the surface that in some aspects of her life she was very stuck and she could no longer ignore those aspects. She was ready to explore the issues around her traumatic childhood that she had buried deep down. It was in therapy that she continued her road to healing from the childhood experiences.

This was a powerful example of where coaching has led to therapy and where both coaching and therapy have changed Maria's life for the better forever.

The dark side of resilience

The current trend in promoting resilience models has a dark side. It sends out the message that we all need to buckle down and just get on with it. But: 'too much resilience can make people overly tolerant of adversity. Just like too much muscle mass can be a bad thing, ie putting a strain on the heart' (Chamorro-Premuzic and Lusk, 2017).

Many of the examples presented in this chapter are from the female lens; however, this is not by any means an indication that only women have these challenges. I have coached and worked with clients across all groups (minority and majority), where the issues discussed here are very relevant.

> 'It is crucial to underscore that this ideal of the resilient woman has coalesced precisely at a time when precarity and inequality are on the rise and as women in the UK are being disproportionately affected by austerity policies. Thus, on the one hand, women's magazines, self-help books, apps, and other media such as reality television and social media platforms offer resources to develop resilience as a way to navigate and survive pain, risk, and difficulties. On the other hand, by promoting elasticity, affirmation and inspiration, the emphasis remains on harnessing individual resources to overcome precarity. Rather than serving to expose and challenge the social and structural sources causing the crisis women experience, these cultural sites are inciting women to work on themselves and assume full responsibility for their well-being. In this way, discussions about the conditions that created precarity and inequality in the first place, and the responsibility of the state and society for addressing them, are effectively silenced.' (Orgad and Gill, 2019)

Understanding the problem with the 'strong black woman' stereotype

Women with an African-Caribbean heritage have historically had the intersectional disadvantage of racism, inequality and social exclusion. On the other hand, they have also faced the western cultural stereotype of the 'strong black woman'. This has played out over many generations and continues to do so. Results suggest that the 'strong black woman' endorsement is related to depression and anxiety symptoms and loneliness (Liao, Wei and Yin, 2019). Those who internalized the 'strong black woman' schema may be more likely to have more maladaptive perfectionism beliefs, which are associated with low self-compassion and less use of collective coping. In coaching, this can surface as the inner critic voice which is very self-critical, or believing it is a sign of weakness to ask for help. In contrast, adaptive perfectionism is **a healthy type of perfectionism where there is a balance of high standards and a tolerance for imperfections** (Stoltz and Ashby, 2007).

Maladaptive perfectionism also leads to unrealistically high standards, being overly concerned with mistakes, and a perceived discrepancy between one's performance and personal standards. These clients may also be at a risk of negative mental health because they tend to equate perfect performance with self-worth, view imperfect performance as a personal failure and focus on the negative aspects of their performance. This is further correlated with depression and anxiety. In turn, these are associated with negative mental health outcomes. Thus, focusing on the development of prevention through coaching is a powerful way of supporting and targeting the 'strong black woman schema' a critical step towards the goal of improving the mental health of African-Caribbean women.

In the UK, the children of the 'Windrush generation', whose parents arrived from Jamaica in the 1950s and 1960s, have had their own challenges of exclusion and racism in education and the workplace.

These second and third generation children often report that they feel it is self-indulgent to share their woes. The typical reasoning behind this is that they have had an easier life because of the sacrifices their parents made. A common feeling is one of guilt. There is a systemic ancestral consciousness that they should be grateful for all they have and there are reminders of family who are still struggling with survival and extreme poverty.

For many the 'strong black woman' stereotype has come with a heavy price and is a double-edged sword. On the one hand, being strong, showing grit, determination and independence on the surface seems powerful. However, these women report that they struggle with celebrating their achievements and are overly self-critical. They are taught from an early age to hide any pain or anger. Many women have lived with the shadow side of the 'strong black woman' stereotype all their lives.

Seeking out transformational coaching can be a life-changing opportunity to be released from the shackles of feeling the need to always show strength regardless of the situation. Tamara Winfrey-Harris says:

> I am not sure that the 'strong black woman' is dead. But she should be. And it is black women who must kill her. Others are far too invested in her survival. For black women, the most radical thing we can do is to throw off the shackles forged by the stereotype and regain our full and complex humanity – one that allows us to be capable, strong, and independent, but also to be carried and cared for ourselves. Allowing for physical and emotional vulnerability is not weakness; it is humanness. More, it is a revolutionary act in the face of a society eager to mould us into hard, unbreakable things.

Resilience can be maladaptive in those situations where it is masking vulnerability or prevents effective action to support someone who could be at risk. Psychological resilience has a paradox: the more resilient someone is, the more likelihood of eventual vulnerability. In particular contexts, the concept of becoming more resilient from the perspective of those from an advantageous group can be misguidedly deployed to further accept disparity and inequality towards those from disadvantaged minority groups. Its message to those who face bias and lack equity is further assigning their sole responsibility to change their life (Mahdiani and Ungar, 2021).

We can reflect on the lived experience of someone who has been labelled as 'strong', where in reality the back story is that due to circumstances there was no other choice but to be resilient. Staying strong, keeping going even when the alarm bells are ringing loudly, places a risk to mental and physical health. A consequence of this is that an individual may struggle to express their true emotions. They may also struggle with self-care and self-compassion. All of this and more is necessary for emotional health and wellbeing.

Being resilient is not useful if deep down it is not serving you or your client. Here are some examples of behavioural situations where during coaching someone may present themselves as strong and resilient on the surface, however paradoxically they are struggling behind the scenes:

- No matter how stressed and burnt out, they are more likely to put up with the situation and keep going in a toxic work culture.

- They are overly conscientious and have difficulty saying 'No'.

- In private they may have given up on themselves and have accepted that things won't get any better.

- They may come across as a bit of a mystery, to cover up their true feelings they have a cheery front but keep others at a distance.

- Deep down they are living with a constant feeling that the system is working against them.

- They may come across as if they have a 'chip' on their shoulder.

- They can be sceptical and cynical.

- They are often perceived as high performers and others take advantage of the fact that they are strong and give them extra work.

- No one ever checks in to see if they are ok because the assumption is that they are strong and independent and therefore don't need anyone.

- Despite being very busy there is a lack of meaningful joy about life and their purpose.

- They ignore or are in denial of their own negative emotions.

- They can be defensive and mistrusting.

- May have occasional emotional outbursts.

- They are just keeping going although there is no end goal.

- Being strong and resilient is the daily norm and not just when a challenge surfaces.

- Being described as strong feels like a burden and not a compliment.

Coaching unhelpful resilience

For those who have had a life where there is no choice but to be strong as a survival strategy, letting go of their protective armour isn't going to be easy. Mostly likely, behind the armour there is someone hiding their fragility. Coaching always needs to be supportive, empathetic and psychologically safe and never more so than in this situation.

It is also worth considering how the client has ended up being coached by you. Someone who has chosen to search out coaching may be in a very different emotional state in comparison to an employee who has been sent for coaching by HR or as part of a development plan. Many organizations have internal coaching pools where the employee is assigned a coach and there is no chemistry session or the opportunity to choose which coach they want to work with. Or, alternatively, the types of coaches they can work with feel limited. If they have been sent by HR or nominated by their manager they may also be feeling concerned that they needed coaching because they weren't good enough or that there is something wrong with them. There is an additional concern that they may also be feeling judged, inadequate and psychologically unsafe. For a client who is used to showing up publicly as strong and resilient, building trust may take time and the coach will need to be patient.

This is another reason why we need both internal coaching pools and external coaches who are typically contracted to work with senior executive leaders. Someone who is from an under-represented minority group may feel more comfortable and psychologically safer opening up to a coach from a similar background. It doesn't mean they will always choose to be coached by someone similar to them, however the option needs to be on the table.

For the resilient client, for whom being stoically strong is a lifetime habit which is no longer serving their growth and emotional health, their coaching journey will be about letting go and sharing what is happening deep down. In this case, there is a strong likelihood of many emotions surfacing which have previously been bottled and stifled. Allowing themselves to be vulnerable isn't something they are used to and comfortable with.

The coach themselves also needs to have the capacity to deal with the very strong emotions which may surface and create the space for these emotions to be contained and safely explored. It is also important that the coach doesn't find themselves creating a dependency. One of the key foundations of coaching as a profession is that our clients aren't 'broken' or 'need fixing'. Coaching is a peer-to-peer relationship where the belief is that with the coach's support our clients have the ability to find their own most appropriate answers.

Coaches need to be mindful that they don't fall into the trap of wanting to rescue their clients or adopt a manner of feeling sorry for them. Both these attitudes are unhelpful and may perpetuate an energy (albeit unintentionally) that the client is helpless, to be pitied and needs saving. This may also come across as disempowering, patronizing and condescending.

From the coach's perspective, they need to remember they are not responsible for the client's actions and outcomes. This always lies with the client and should be agreed as part of the contracting work together. What the coach can do is champion what the client does well and build from there.

COACHING 'DEFENSIVENESS' AND RESILIENCE

For many clients, who have learnt to hold everything together and keep everything under wraps, allowing themselves to open up will be an alien and deeply uncomfortable experience. It can leave them feeling nervous, exposed and vulnerable. They may unconsciously want to steer the coach towards a superficial transactional coaching session. Although we as coaches always meet our clients where they are we also need to be mindful that in this situation we don't end up coaching the client's survival side or their inner critic. It may take several sessions before they really open up to us.

They are also likely to be cognitively and emotionally exhausted.

Although the following technique can apply to all coaching scenarios it works especially well to help a client be 'present' and 'open up'. It is a great way to start a powerful coaching session, especially if someone tends to always show up with their strong resilient side.

Imagine you are about to coach someone who comes across as stoic and determined. They are constantly spinning many plates, yet their body language is tense, rigid and closed. Your sense is that they aren't fully connected with their emotions or what they are feeling. Your instinct tells you they may need a few minutes to slow down and be present before the coaching can begin.

Some coaches like to use Tibetan singing bowls at the start of the coaching session. When they strike the bowl, the sound triggers theta brainwave frequencies which then stimulate clarity of mind, by quietening the distractions of the outside world and therefore creating a bridge to the present moment. In a corporate setting this can be very impactful and shift their energy. The whole exercise takes less than a minute.

Other powerful ways to coach someone who may be struggling with their feelings and emotions is to say something like:

'Take a breather'

'Would it help to take a deep breath?'

(Coach breathes in with the client)
Followed with questions such as:

'What are you feeling right now?'

'What is going on for you?'

'Where do you feel that in your body?'

The breath itself can help make the transition into the coaching session by quietening the mental chatter and creating space for deeper explorative work. Note that these sentences don't always have to be at the beginning of the coaching. They can be said at any stage during the coaching if strong emotions surface. Authentic resilience is cultivated from healthy positive emotions.

Who is this information useful for?

All coaches need to be aware that a client who seems very resilient, and has had a complex lived experience of adversity, may actually be showing 'dysfunctional resilience' as in reality they are close to burn-out or feeling emotionally depleted. What is required in this instance is deep empathy, emotional safety and active listening.

The following questions carry far more weight:

- How can I support you?
- Would you like to continue talking about what's happened?
- What do you need to let go of?
- What does being strong mean to you?
- What are the costs to always having to be the strong one?
- How can you move forward from this with self-care and self-compassion?
- If you stopped doing this, what would be possible?

Reframing resilience

Resilience isn't about being strong: it's about knowing when to quit, move on and let go. Perseverance is an admirable quality but, in some circumstances, the most powerful thing to do is to accept that changing direction may be for the best. For someone who has had to 'be strong' to survive, they may need to revisit and reframe their personal relationship with what it means to be resilient and actually explore how they can allow themselves to be vulnerable yet still feel psychologically safe. Coaching may require fostering their psychological safety so they can allow themselves to be vulnerable.

Here are some tips on how to coach a client who needs to embrace vulnerability:

- Clients work at their own speed so don't be tempted to push them to open up and be vulnerable. Instead focus on creating emotional safety, building trust and rapport.
- Our clients may not realize they are coming across as defensive and closed. There may be an opportunity to coach around their level of self-awareness.
- Agree a task where they could ask someone to help in an area they are struggling.

- Try a 'future self' exercise, looking at how they see themselves in the twilight of their life. How will they feel at this time? Who will be with them? How did they get there? What was their life like along the way? These are all very powerful questions which help a client to deeply reflect not just on the actions they need to take but how they want to feel along the journey of their life. It's by accessing our innermost feelings that we open ourselves up for the deeper work.

- Be curious about unmet needs. What have they learnt to tolerate to stay strong?

- Let them know you have their back and be their safety net as they learn to take the steps towards being vulnerable.

Reflective work

Coaching someone who has learnt to be strong and resilient may lead to you needing to support them on the journey to letting their guard down, opening up and being more vulnerable. In this reflective exercise, I want you to connect with your own vulnerability.

We have all at some point in our lives faced a situation in which we didn't feel safe or have the capacity to show up as our real selves. Perhaps the situation had or has become so toxic that you don't even know how to open up yourself.

Even if you know this might be to your detriment, you still don't want to or feel that you have capacity to be more open. From this fearful and closed place, you are not free to express your feelings or show any vulnerability.

Can you think of a situation or relationship where you have to stay guarded, however you have no choice but to carry on regardless of how you were feeling inside, past or present?

- What is that situation? Or who is that person?
- How does it feel when you think about it?
- Where in your body do you feel that sensation?

- What would it be like if you had to let go of that fear and let that person in or enter the situation from a more open perspective?

- What could be the worst that could happen?

- What would stop you in your tracks from taking action or speaking up?

- What needs to be in place for you emotionally and practically to take the risk and be more open?

- What does being vulnerable feel like?

- Based on this exercise, what have you learnt about yourself that could support you in being more empathetic in your coaching?

References

Blume, J (1970) *Are You There God? It's Me Margaret*, Pan Macmillan, London

Chamorro-Premuzic, T and Lusk, D (2017) The dark side of resilience, *Harvard Business Review*, August

Liao, K Y-H, Wei, M and Yin, M (2019) The misunderstood schema of the strong black woman: exploring its mental health consequences and coping responses among African American women, *Psychology of Women Quarterly,* 44 (1), 84–104, doi.org/10.1177%2F0361684319883198 (archived at perma.cc/NU4X-WW5D)

Mahdiani, H and Ungar, M (2021) The dark side of resilience, *Adversity and Resilience Science*, 2, 147–155, doi.org/10.1007/s42844-021-00031-z (archived at perma.cc/N55U-AXV5)

Miguel, D R (1997) *The Four Agreements: A Practical Guide to Personal Freedom*, Amber-Allen Publishing, San Rafael, CA

Orgad, S and Gill, R (2019) The limits of the 'resilient woman' ideal, *LSE Business Review*, blogs.lse.ac.uk/businessreview/2019/07/01/the-limits-of-the-resilient-woman-ideal/ (archived at perma.cc/ZJ2F-QNPX)

Salinger, J D (1961) *Franny and Zooey*, Little, Brown, New York

Stoltz, K and Ashby S J (2007) Perfectionism and lifestyle: personality differences among adaptive perfectionists, maladaptive perfectionists, and nonperfectionists, *Journal of Individual Psychology*, 63 (4) 414–423

Winfrey Harris, T., (2014), 'Precious Mettle: The myth of the strong black woman', BitchMedia, May, www.bitchmedia.org/article/precious-mettle-myth-strong-black-woman (archived at https://perma.cc/6UVW-VB2G)

08

Authenticity

Behaving skilfully and being true to yourself

It is a peculiar sensation, this double-consciousness, this sense of always looking at one's self through the eyes of others, of measuring one's soul by the tape of a world that looks on in amused contempt and pity.

W E B DU BOIS, *THE SOULS OF BLACK FOLK* (1903)

The constant bombardment of messages around the desire for authentic leadership, that showing up as our true selves is the secret to living our best life, has entered the current zeitgeist of workplace culture. And that by us being our true selves and authentic, while occupying private and professional roles, it can give us an elevated sense of power and is beneficial to our wellbeing too (Gan, Heller and Chen, 2018).

Conversely, for most of us to progress in careers or to be accepted in certain groups we have had to conform to fit in: from hiding important aspects of our identity to editing and only showing those parts of ourselves that are psychologically safe to express openly. The reality is that there is a huge pressure to dress, behave, speak and look a certain way to fit in with the dominant culture at work and our surroundings.

Being our true selves and revealing the real authentic part of us comes at a risk. Prior to training as a coach, I worked in the tech sector. Despite qualifying as a coach in my personal time, I had to keep under wraps my growing interest in wanting to help others to flourish and grow. The culture I worked in viewed altruism and kindness as a weakness and instead rewarded large egos, competitiveness, and dog-eat-dog behaviour to get ahead. Most of the qualities were in sharp contrast to my own values, beliefs and temperament.

For many, the advice and rhetoric around authenticity feels precarious and confusing. There is a cognitive dissonance in that on one hand we are told to be our true selves; yet there is also a potential penalty in the workplace from having a certain hairstyle, alternative lifestyle choice, wearing a hijab, a crucifix, or speaking with an accent. This can result in being or feeling indirectly forced to make a choice between career, identity and transparency.

For someone from an under-represented minority group to be told they must now be totally authentic, this can actually trip them up. For example, an individual openly sharing their experiences of racism, homophobia or sexism, only to be met with microaggressions or a rebuke that their lived experience is subjective or simply not true is enough to make anyone revert to only sharing the edited version of themselves.

I have worked with many clients who have paid the penalty for speaking their truth, leading to confusion and further disconnect. For someone from an under-represented minority group this can be emotionally taxing especially if their values and cultural backgrounds are very different from the majority group.

What do coaches need to understand?

The rewards of feeling free and empowered, to not have to hide and pretend or be someone we are not just to survive and get along, can be personally momentous. As coaches we are in a privileged position to support someone to live in the flow of their authenticity. However, firstly we need to get under the skin to consider why, for someone from an under-represented minority group, this journey has considerably many more layers of complexity. Coaches need to understand the risk a client may face in being their true self: exploring how they could cope with being misunderstood. They need to lean into the ugly truth that despite organizations talking about inclusion, there is also a powerful systemic desire for everyone to conform to the majority culture. Our clients from under-represented minority groups have been living with the paradox of what it means to be authentic and the pressure to fit in for most of their lives. The case study below is an example of this.

CASE STUDY: CLARE

Clare is an NHS coach and trainer; she describes herself as white British gay. She is in her 50s and lives in Sussex with her partner and child. This is what she says:

'I was born in the late 1960s into a white English, staunchly working-class background in a northern English industrial town. My mum was not in a relationship with my birth father. My stepdad had mental health issues which led to me being sent to live with my grandparents at the age of two. I was mainly raised by my grandma, as my grandad died when I was seven. Although my mum was in my life, she lived in another city so, growing up, I did not consider her my true parent. Even now, if I am honest with myself, my grandma was and always will be my mum. I feel this is very important to mention, because the experience of growing up in that place in those days, in a non-conventional family, is quite important in my early perception of being different. I guess even before I started realizing that my sexuality wasn't normal (as was the belief back then) I already felt like a bit of an outsider.

I always knew I was different. From being very young I didn't quite feel that I fitted in. When my mum bought me a Tiny Tears doll when I was about eight, I was truly disappointed because what I really wanted was an Action Man. I ended up filling the doll with water and using her as a large unwieldy water pistol. I hated wearing dresses. I didn't like how they made me feel and hated the attention I got. People always say girls are pretty in dresses and I hated that; possibly because I didn't want the attention. I already felt strange not being in a normal family. I only knew one other kid in a single-parent family. It was really strange to many that I was also an only child – virtually all my friends at primary school (and come to think of it secondary school too) had siblings. It always felt like people pitied me because I didn't have a dad and didn't live with my mum. This did feel strange and I did sometimes envy friends who lived with their mum and dad – although I loved my grandma very much. The sense of pity prevailed and sort of became a mind-set. When people did nice stuff for me it kind of felt that they were doing it because they felt sorry for me. It took me a long time – probably when I was in my 30s – to realize that my life was good because I was good and not because people were giving me a break.

I became known, and strongly identified, as a tomboy (I suppose gender non-conforming would be the label today). To be clear, I never actually wanted to be a boy. I just liked to do boy stuff like climb trees and play football. This is more a comment on the time that I grew up, and the fact that my grandma had Victorian views. Gender roles were pretty concrete in the 70s and there wasn't much flexibility in people's opinions of how a girl should be. I think some of my awkwardness with myself was as much to do with this rigid societal view of how women should act and behave than my sexuality. I rebelled against this and, by and large, my family accepted that I was 'different'. When I was 11 my favourite ABBA song was (and probably still is) 'That's Me'. I already knew that I didn't want to marry a man. I wasn't ready to think about being with a girl but I knew that I was different.

Teenage years

I am not sure when I first started to realize that I was gay but it does feel like it has always been there. I did not feel able to embrace this for a long time. I always felt different from my peers and preferred not to think about how that made me feel. I think it was when I was about 13 that I started fancying girls and it was very scary. I felt like a freak and tended to bury the feelings. Lesbians were particularly invisible back then. There was a great deal of homophobia but this tended to be aimed at men. I felt right through secondary school that I had a dirty secret that I could never share and this made me feel all kind of emotions from physically sick, to unhappy and scared. My deepest fear back then was that someone would find out about who I really was, so I buried it deep and refused to think about it.

Early adult years

In the late 80s I moved to London to train to be a nurse. I can still remember buying my first *Time Out* magazine and furtively scanning the gay section. I think moving to London was the best thing that ever happened to me. It was still a bumpy road, particularly in the early days, but I made friends and felt that I had found my tribe. Most of the people I met had exclusively gay female friends. The scene was amazing and just what I needed but it was, back then, very separatist. Most female gay spaces were women-only with a few allowing men only as guests. I remember a massive furore happening one night in a women-only bar in a lesbian and gay centre when the only person free to work was a male bar tender. I felt so sorry for him and was very nice to him when some others even refused to be served by him. I started to realize that I had spent most of my life feeling a little off-centre and wanting inclusion and here I was in the promised land being part of a system that seemed to exclude others.

Coming out was like being freed from a cage I had been in for as long as I could remember. I started to tell my friends on my nursing course, one at a time, starting with those I felt were not going to freak out. Most of them were fine. Some were not, but I guess I had to accept that some people would never accept gay people. I remember one so-called friend telling me that it was unnatural and I should admit that I was not normal. I started realizing that people would stop talking as I came into the room and, although that sick frightened feeling came back on occasion, it never stayed too long. The truth was that I had a core of about four friends who stood by me and protected me. All heterosexual, but all cared for my welfare and had my back. I am still good friends with two of them to this day and will always be so grateful that they stood by me.

I then realized that I needed to tell my friends back home. I went back up North and one by one met up with them and told them. They all stood by me. Most of them had their suspicions already. Some of them were just relieved that I was ok because they had found me distant for a while and were worried. My mum was initially shocked, but she too accepted me and has never said anything negative. She hasn't always liked my girlfriends but that is just being a mum, I think.

When it comes to thinking about inclusion, LGBTQ+ rights and societal attitudes are so much better today. In some communities there are still a lot of people struggling but it is so much better than it was. Back in the early 1990s every single gay pub had blacked-out windows or was in a basement. It felt like we were hidden away. Life still felt like we were keeping secrets. You always looked left and right before entering a bar in case someone was looking. Heckling and lewd comments were always a risk, usually from heterosexual men. Gay men were the target of violence more but rape threats towards lesbians were not unheard of – although I am glad to say that never happened to me personally.

One thing that has prevailed throughout my life, and still happens on occasion, is the assumption that I am heterosexual: from the family doctor who repeatedly tried to get me to take the oral contraceptive pill at the age of 16, to the practice nurse who told me that I could still get pregnant when I was 50. One memorable occasion was the patient who held up the front page of a tabloid paper with a photo of the previous day's Pride gay parade – complete with homophobic headline – and said to me, 'Look at those perverts'. I quickly scanned the photo with my heart pounding in my ears, mouth going dry and feeling sick, to see if I was there. Even if I had been I don't think the person would have made the connection. I was a nice nurse in a uniform so I couldn't be one of them. I then realized that it was that person's problem.

Heteronormative assumptions are everywhere in society – even now. Being lesbian is particularly prone to this. Add to that being a parent and it gets even more entrenched. When my partner and I decided we wanted to be parents I had all kinds of fears. I was worried that our child would be bullied because they had two mums. Worried that we would be ostracized and avoided in the playground. Even concerned that the child might hate us because we are not a normal family. I am so happy to say the opposite was true. Our child got through the teenage years completely happy and settled with two mums. All his friends are aware and didn't particularly seem to find it strange, apart from the odd occasions of the 'you can't be his mum – that other woman is' variety which, if I am totally honest, were far more embarrassing for the person who got the situation wrong. We made friends in the playground with some people that we will remain friends with long after the school days are over. Some parents looked sideways at us, but then we looked sideways at others. Nobody can be friends with everyone they meet and that is the way the world is.

How have the experiences above affected me in the long run?

I guess the word that comes to mind is resilience. I grew up too afraid of what people thought of me and was ashamed of who I was. Through a number of life experiences and, notably, the experience of coming out and not losing any friends or family, I became very comfortable and proud of who I am. This did not happen overnight and there have been plenty of times when my sexuality made me unhappy and uncomfortable. The bottom line is, though, I found the strength to push back against society's views on how I should live and was able to believe in myself and, above all, love myself. This gave me the strength to strive for happiness. I believe I am one of the lucky ones. I know gay, trans and lesbian people who lost their friends and family. I became, and am, very comfortable in my skin and do not hide my sexuality from anyone. I feel very grateful to have my partner and son and am very happy.

What would I say to my younger self?

When I was 13, I would have given anything to be 'normal'. If you had offered me a pill that would have made me feel about a boy the way I felt about girls I would have taken two! If I could go back and speak to my younger self, I would give her a big hug and tell her that however hopeless life seemed then, amazing times will definitely come. I would tell myself to stop worrying, that I would have a happy life with a lovely wife and that I would also be a mum – something at that time I just could not picture. Most of all I would tell me to just believe in myself and that everything was going to work out just fine.

How has it manifested in the workplace?

I am very aware of how challenging life can be for anyone who is different. I feel very grateful to be living in a time and place where I am free to live as I choose. I always support the underdog because, despite where I am now, I did feel like that was me for a very long time. I am out at work but that is very easy because I am very senior now. The lower down the ranks (in any job) the easier it is to allow the fear of not fitting in, and bullying, to prevent you being yourself. I know not everybody likes the fact I am gay but, to be honest, I couldn't care less'.

Key points to note from Clare's story:

We meet Clare at a time in her life where she is thriving. She has a happy family life, is successful in her career and at peace with the challenges she has overcome to get to this place. It is important to point out that it became easier for Clare to be open about her sexuality once she was in a very senior role. Power and position play an instrumental role in our confidence to be ourselves, without any penalties or repercussions. However, there is also much to learn about how some of her earlier challenges may have surfaced during coaching.

- On a number of occasions, she had a physical reaction of feeling sick at the thought of people finding out she is gay. We may need to support a client with breathing exercises, similar to the ones in Chapter 7 on resilience, if they start to feel very anxious. The breathing can bring them back to the present rather than becoming overwhelmed about what could happen in the future.

Powerful coaching questions for someone feeling highly anxious could be:

1 Can you change this?

2 Can you accept this?

3 What would be the best-case scenario?

4 What's the worst thing that could happen?

Although, over the years, Clare has realized that the prejudice is the other person's issue and not hers, this level of self-belief hasn't happened overnight. Dealing with prejudice is hurtful and coaches need to be aware that it can take time for someone to get to a point where they feel empowered enough to not feel impacted by prejudice. Also, it is worth bearing in mind that if our client has experienced prejudice from someone who is in a position of power, this may compound their feelings of worthlessness and low self-esteem.

Powerful coaching questions for someone who has experienced prejudice could be:

1 How did this make you feel?

2 What are your choices?

3 What do you want to do about it?

- The pain of finding out a friend's reaction when you share yourself completely may mean that some friends will leave your life and others you will need to let go. A client may need support during coaching around this change in friendship and their wider support circles.

Powerful coaching questions for someone whose friendships are changing:

1 What do you need from friends?

2 What would you be losing if you ended this friendship?

3 What would you gain from letting go of this friend?

4 Do you feel supported by your friend?

5 Does your friend bring you joy?

- Leading a double or secret life is not being inauthentic, it is often due to circumstances and the reality of someone's life and lived experience. As coaches, we need to be open, accepting and non-judgemental about someone who has a secret or double life. Our clients belong to many systems and will have hidden loyalties towards some more than others. These loyalties can feel confusing, especially when a client is trying to figure out their identity or their place in a system. For Clare, it was figuring out how she fitted into the LGBTQ+ community, and which rules she was and wasn't comfortable following as a member of that community. Coaches should not unwittingly imply that it isn't 'right' to have a secret life or that it is inauthentic. Instead, be empathetic and open to the challenges and frustrations of our client's feeling that they have no choice in the matter.

Powerful coaching questions for someone who feels they have to keep aspects of their life hidden:

1 What would your ideal situation look like?

2 How do you manage the emotional side of keeping things hidden?

3 What is working right now?

4 What aspects are you struggling with?

5 What do you want to do about it?

- A lack of support from a colleague who didn't believe her relationship breakdown was a painful experience brought an awareness that her personal lived experience was being belittled and minimized. Coaches need to be careful not to shut down a conversation where a client has felt this way.

Powerful coaching questions for someone who feels misunderstood or dismissed by others:

1 What did you need from your colleague at that time?

2 How did their comments made you feel?

3 What would you do differently next time?

4 What do you need to accept?

5 What do you need to let go of?

Code-switching and coaching

There are some friends I greet with both arms stretched out with a big bear hug, some with a peck on both cheeks, while others are greeted with a warm handshake and everything else in between. The type of greeting is pretty much reflected by my relationship with that person, the context of the situation plus my reading of the receiver's physical boundaries. It appears I'm in good company as in 2012, when President Barack Obama met the US men's Olympic basketball team, the way he greeted the black NBA player Kevin Durant with a cross-body shoulder handshake was very different from the conventional handshake with the white assistant coach. This greeting went viral and was an excellent example of code-switching.

Code-switching is a practice common to under-represented minority groups of changing or editing their communication style, appearance and behaviour to fit in or feel accepted. For many, the need to subtly change how they express themselves linguistically and behaviourally is a well-honed survival skill. Nevertheless, it can be emotionally exhausting to tone down an accent or figure out the etiquette rules for fine dining when eating out with clients at a corporate event. The more someone moves into a leadership role, the more the concept of being professional at work is synonymous with behaving and looking in a way which is more aligned to the majority group. Treading the line with regard to fitting in, by constantly code-switching, can cause anxiety and high levels of stress.

From another angle, the skill to naturally code-switch can open doors and, in some instances, might even save your life. Before the age of five I could speak English, Punjabi and Urdu. On many occasions, being able to express myself in three languages has come in extremely useful and humorous and has got me out of many a tricky situation when I'm with someone who can switch the codes with me. With that in mind it can be empowering. The challenge arises and can be emotionally exhausting when I have to code-switch just to fit in.

What do coaches need to know?

Coaches need to be aware of certain issues about code-switching.

- That it exists and some clients may be code-switching unconsciously as well as consciously. Our role is not to judge, educate or guide our clients towards whether they should code-switch or not. We need to stand in the truth of the code-switching reality for many from under-represented groups.

- Be curious about the impact and whether code-switching is serving our clients or stopping them living in the flow of their lives. We don't even have to use the term code-switching – just simply be aware that it exists.

- Code-switching comes with the potential rewards of social mobility, physical safety and security. The ability to modify and change to benefit ourselves can also be summed up as 'cultural capital'.

- Some clients from under-represented groups may be code-switching during the coaching with you, especially if there is a wide disparity between the coach and client due to social class, race etc.

- If the client is having to code-switch to fit in, or make an impression during coaching, this will be emotionally exhausting and there is a significant chance the coaching will be superficial. It may be an idea to coach them away from their work environment. How does that make you feel as a coach? What can you do to create psychological safety?

- Clients may have to pay a penalty for not code-switching. Many organizations make bold statements around how they don't ask their employees to change; however, cultural norms can be deeply entrenched and are implicit. Be open to the fact that your client may have had many negative experiences because they do not know how to code-switch or simply refused to. For example, this might include missing out on promotion, not being invited into high-profile meetings or not assigned critical projects.

- It is worth exploring if the client doesn't know how to code-switch or has decided not to.

- The idea of 'just being yourself' is a misnomer without understanding the dynamic of privilege and power interplaying. In the case study, Clare found it much easier and safer to be open about her sexuality the more senior she has become in the organization.

- There are also many benefits to code-switching. Just as we discussed healthy self vs survival self in Chapter 6 on trauma, there is healthy code-switching vs survival code-switching. Healthy code-switching is when someone is flexing their behaviour, dress and language in an empowered way and does not feel they are putting on an act or being fake to be accepted. There is a natural ease and control in the situation. Survival code-switching is having to put on an act because the consequences of not changing are dire and could lead to exclusion, microaggression, prejudice or have career-limiting ramifications. It is our clients who decide the line between what is healthy code-switching vs survival code-switching for them.

COACHING FOR AUTHENTICITY

In a perfect world it would be wonderful if each one of us could be 100 per cent authentic 100 per cent of the time. However, that in itself is unrealistic. It is extremely difficult to be truly authentic if we don't feel comfortable or safe. The result of having to constantly code-switch can mean that in some respects you may have lost a sense of who you truly are.

One of the gifts of coaching is helping our clients to strengthen their sense of self, with the voice to say, 'this is the real me, this is my truth and I'm ok with it'. The following are examples of powerful coaching questions to help a client explore their authentic self:

- When do you feel the most authentic?
- Who are you with when you feel your best?
- Who brings out the worst in you?
- How does that make you feel?
- Which activities make you feel alive and joyful?
- What is it about those activities that makes you feel so positive?
- Who do you need to let go to feel more authentic?
- What do you need to stop doing to feel more authentic?
- What kind of people do you have difficulty saying 'No' to?

- Which situations make you feel very uncomfortable?
- Could you look at these in a different way?
- How can you be more professional at work without compromising your authenticity?

The vast majority of coaching clients do not set out to be inauthentic or deliberately give a false impression. It certainly is not our role as coaches to adjudicate if someone is being authentic or not. Our role is to support our clients to figure out what authenticity means to them. I have facilitated hundreds of coaching workshops around the topic of 'Building your personal brand'. My approach to this work is always inside-out, starting with an exploration of personal core values, purpose, dreams and goals. These exercises inevitably raise questions around personal values vs cultural values or family values, and letting go of belief systems that no longer serve who they really are.

Once this deeper work is done, people can move on to the actions that they need to take to meet their goals. Once the participants are connected to their values, they feel confident and empowered to 'behave skilfully' in order to reach their desired goals. This behaving skilfully may mean acquiring healthy code-switching skills or deciding to let go of survival code-switching. Authenticity is a lifelong process and requires courage, grit and determination – all of which is very possible in coaching.

Reflective work

- Can you think of a time you had to change how you dressed or spoke to fit in and be accepted?
- Have you ever had to hide some aspect of your life so you don't feel judged, rejected or excluded by others? How did you feel on those occasions?
- Would you change that now?
- What was the cost and what was the benefit?

If you are someone who has never felt pressurised or had the need to code-switch to get along in your career, education, socially with friendship groups, be accepted by your neighbours and so on, consider the following:

- In your circle of professional and personal networks what observable examples of code-switching in others have you come across?
- How can you build your empathy to understand what it's like for someone who has to code-switch to feel accepted and included?
- What are your biases around cultural norms?
- How can you step up and be an ally?
- What does the phrase, 'I'm not racist because I don't see colour' mean to you?
- What if a person of colour told you that, by not seeing their colour, you were not seeing all of them?

References

Du Bois W E B (1903) *The Souls of Black Folk: Essays and sketches*, Oxford World Classics, Oxford

Gan, M, Heller, D and Chen, S (2018) The power in being yourself: feeling authentic enhances the sense of power, *Personality and Social Psychology Bulletin*, 44 (10), 1460–1472

09

Psychological safety

Being vs feeling psychologically safe

I've learned that people will forget what you said, people will forget what you did, but people will never forget how you made them feel.

MAYA ANGELOU

In order to open up and bring the real issue to the coaching session, the coach needs to cultivate psychological safety. When a client doesn't feel psychologically safe, they shut down from opening up completely. They edit what they share and leave the session feeling it was superficial and a waste time of time.

Being safe is not the same as feeling psychologically safe. Feeling psychologically safe within ourselves is an instinctive gut feeling that we are emotionally safe. Psychological safety is at the heart of our sense of belonging, feeling included, thriving and living our best life. It means we can be ourselves and speak up without fear of being ridiculed, shamed, talked down to, ostracized, ganged up on, judged, talked over, ignored, excluded or rejected.

We carried out a poll on LinkedIn asking the question:

'What do you feel is the most important factor that plays to you having a sense of belonging in a workplace situation?'

Your voice is heard	28 per cent
Feeling seen	5 per cent
Psychological safety	51 per cent
Fairness and equity	16 per cent

I want you to read this chapter from the wider systemic lens of coaching someone who has a complex biography of experiences that have often left them feeling psychologically unsafe. This could be because of their race, gender, religion, sexuality, disability or social class, culture or family of origin.

A client I worked with recalled her first day in a new role for a large corporate organization. Unknown to her, the manager who had hired her was now on gardening leave and she never saw him again. There was no on-boarding or support in terms of role expectations or project assignment. She was pretty much left floundering. Much later she found out that a few individuals in the department had already decided that she wasn't up to the role and rumours spread that she was incompetent and a poor hire. That was, until someone else in the team could see what was going on and knew from her own experience that she had been neglected and poorly managed. This person decided to take her under her wing and support her in getting the information she needed to get on with the job.

Other kinder colleagues, who had been through a similar experience, also took her to one side and gave her some survival tips on dealing with the politics. Things eventually improved with the appointment of a new director and the exit of the people who had tried to discredit her. Unfortunately, this dysfunctional behaviour was systemic and positively rewarded, and they all manoeuvred themselves into different departments, promotions and pay rises.

From every conceivable angle this organization was the antithesis of psychological safety. There were secret alliances and covering for others, while using positions to withhold information or getting others to selectively pass on information. There were also ways of intimidating by excluding her from team meetings and high-profile projects.

With the added layers of my client being a minority person, from a working-class background in a very male-dominated organization, as well as being the only Asian in the department, it was no surprise that she had to work hard at faking her confidence to hide the fact she felt very psychologically unsafe and threatened the whole time. She shared how throughout her ten-year career, despite promotion, she had never felt completely psychologically safe working for that organization. In order to survive she quickly learnt how to navigate the toxic landscape. Nevertheless, she certainly didn't have a sense of belonging – this was a culture where people survived instead of thrived. This was far removed from bringing your best self to work.

Much has been written about the many benefits of psychological safety in the workplace, including higher performance, innovation and profitability. Dr Amy Edmondson (1999) defined psychological safety as 'a shared belief held by members of a team that the team is safe for interpersonal risk-taking'. That means it is ok to speak up without the fear of being punished, ridiculed or humiliated. Also, that it is perfectly all right to make mistakes. Psychological safety is an innate feeling that there is no threat or harm to our mental wellbeing. It is also important to acknowledge that a lack of psychological safety for those from under-represented groups carries a far heavier and multi-layered penalty.

To believe there is one solution to living a psychologically safe life forever more is wishful thinking and unrealistic. Despite the growing interest in this area, which is positive and encouraging, we have to accept that psychological safety is not binary, but more of a sliding scale, depending on the context and our wider systemic experiences. For coaches, this means developing an understanding, empathy and awareness of our client's prior experiences of feeling psychologically safe and an acceptance that despite our efforts it may take a lot longer for some people to feel safe.

The 1:1 coaching seesaw of psychological safety

Psychological and emotional safety are non-negotiables for masterful coaching, both from the perspective of the coach and the client. Think of this as the seesaw in a children's playground, which requires one child on either end for balance and co-ordination. Creating a feeling of psychological safety between a coach and client is also a fragile balancing act of empathy, trust, courage, respect and vulnerability.

With a seesaw, a clumsy exit of one child at the bottom of the seesaw can send the other one hurtling upwards with the potential of dangerously coming off and getting hurt. Similarly, during coaching, if either party does not feel psychologically or emotionally safe this will inevitably have a negative impact on the overall quality of the coaching intervention. Creating and nurturing psychological safety needs patience and time. Some clients will take longer to get there, while others may never open up entirely and the coaching will be transactional and not transformational. As coaches, we always meet our clients where they are. It must always be about our client's journey and not our own ego.

Most coaches care deeply about their clients and want to do their best in creating psychological safety during coaching. As psychological safety in this context is a 'feeling', we as coaches cannot control, suggest or tell our clients how they should be feeling.

I am always incredibly humbled when a client or a team feel psychologically safe to open up and share their lived experience. By respecting and listening to their stories we are opening the door to deeper, more meaningful work.

As explored in the next case study, a client may have had many past experiences of feeling vulnerable and exposed, such that feeling emotionally unsafe has become their day-to-day norm rather than an occasional feeling.

The following story is about Sara, a 36-year-old coach and business partner.

CASE STUDY: SARA

Sara describes herself as Black British and was born in Scotland to parents from East Africa. Both her parents arrived in the UK in the 1980s with scholarships to attend university. Sara was born soon afterwards. Her father decided to move back to Africa while her mother stayed and raised Sara and her sister as a single parent. She describes her mum as a 'big' personality while her father wasn't very hands on. Sara grew up in a very white community in Scotland and between the ages of two and nine her mother left both Sara and her older sister with a white foster family while she moved to another city to find work. During that period Sara's mother would regularly visit; however, this left Sara feeling irritated and frustrated. Her mother, on the other hand, would be upset at the thought of leaving her daughters while she worked elsewhere.

At nine Sara moved in with her mother, which meant leaving the small white hostile community where she lived for a new life in a large busy cosmopolitan city. This came as a shock; it took Sara a considerable time to adjust and fit in with her fellow street-smart and savvy multi-cultural classmates. Despite the school being culturally diverse, Sara still felt she didn't belong as she didn't sound like the other children, had never come across the music they listened to and couldn't connect with their lifestyles. She felt very judged for being different and 'not cool' by her classmates. At the same time, her mother was putting a lot of pressure on her academically and once again she felt judged and not good enough. Not surprisingly, she was also struggling to emotionally connect with her mother and would regularly ring her foster mother.

At the age of 11, Sara was sent to a predominantly white, middle-class girls-only independent school. Looking back, the school was lovely and her classmates were kind; although once again Sara herself felt very out of place.

Sara is aware that she projected how she was feeling by keeping a distance, and it is something she still does today. Through her coaching she has become aware that to feel safe she chooses to exclude herself. She has always described herself as a private person and is now realizing that she needs to start sharing more of herself to build relationships and connect with others.

She has often not felt safe around people who look like her as their upbringing has been very different. She is very astute at reading a room quickly. On the other hand, when she does feel safe, she can candidly talk about her quirks as long as she is safe in the knowledge that the listener is non-judgemental, receptive and open.

Sara's story isn't uncommon. The roots of her lack of psychological safety are planted in her childhood story, which she had started to address in counselling before she started her coaching. She has well-honed survival strategies of keeping a distance from others and a self-fulfilling narrative around how she is a very private person. Although she has been with her existing employer for many years, and is highly regarded and respected at work, she finds herself hesitating to push herself forward.

When we drilled further down, a similar occurrence to the client story shared earlier emerged. She admitted this was due to an initial very inept on-boarding process and negative experiences when she first joined the organization. This has left her feeling unsafe and knocked her confidence, which is only natural for someone whose childhood experiences of safety are already shaky, through parenting and the schooling system, when starting in an organization where they feel threatened once more.

I have every confidence in Sara that she is doing the work to play the part and fully engage – what needs to happen in her organization is that they meet her halfway and reciprocate by intentionally creating a culture of psychological safety.

Coaching tips for psychological safety

Now, I'll share some tips for coaching someone like Sara who has experienced a lack of psychological safety. My advice is that the coach:

- Must be willing to go at their client's pace.
- Should not ask too many personal questions too soon.
- Should not make assumptions or paraphrase their lived experience.
- Has patience and allows time for the trust to develop.
- Be sensitive to the fact their client has previously felt 'not good enough' and that this feeling should not be repeated during the coaching. One way to get around this would be contracting how to voice the feeling if it does arise during coaching.
- Ensures that the client does not feel judged; again, there could be some contracting around this.
- Should hold the space for the client to process the experience.

- Should be an ally so that the client can feel genuinely safe.
- Should not play the devil's advocate by questioning what happened, as this sends out the message that their experience is imagined and not real.
- Does not use an overly challenging coaching style as it could be unhelpful and could make things worse.
- Should be curious about what the client chooses as a motivation for transformation and self-awareness.

Coaching someone who doesn't feel psychologically safe, particularly if they are from a minority group and has experienced prejudice, will require a great deal of cultural sensitivity and patience. As coaches, we have to acknowledge which clients we serve the best and where we play to our strengths. If you're a coach whose style is to ask prodding, challenging questions that inspire speedy action and fast-moving results, coaching someone who isn't feeling psychologically safe may feel too slow or you may end up having a superficial coaching intervention. Being challenged when they don't feel safe can also leave a person feeling judged and belittled. Building psychological safety takes time and, once the trust is in place, we can ask the challenging questions. It's not a case of not asking the challenging questions: it's about when and how to ask the questions.

The following case study is an example of when a coach can also feel psychologically unsafe if the client raises an issue which feels too uncomfortable.

CASE STUDY: BHAVINI

Bhavini describes herself as a British-born Sri Lankan. She is in her 40s, a pharmacist, married with two children.

Her executive coach, Gillian, came from a recommendation from a friend who had been coached by Gillian in her workplace. Trained with a linear coaching model, Gillian had a fierce reputation for getting results through challenging and powerful questions. Bhavini had initially reached out as she was feeling stuck and trapped in her career and was considering alternative options, including training up to be a coach herself.

They had been working together for a few months when Bhavini arrived at one session feeling shaken up because of something deeply shocking she had discovered a few days back about her school friend. Quite by chance she found out through someone that her friend's husband had been a member of a far-right political party with a manifesto for an ethnically cleansed nation. To her horror, he was quoted on a pamphlet saying he thought there were too many Asians in Britain and that the British culture was being lost.

Bhavini had known him herself for many years and had never known of his real views about Asian families that had moved into the area over time. Having considered the article, she rang her friend the next day for an explanation. Her friend was obviously shocked about the revelation and explained that her husband wasn't really racist. He had joined the party just for a year after a prolonged period of abuse from a few local teenage boys. She asked Bhavini to remember he was a kind, gentle person who was just protecting his family. She avoided the specifics of what he had said.

Gillian, herself a white middle-class coach, had lived most of her life in Winchester and had very little experience of living in a culturally diverse community. Faced with the issue that Bhavini was raising in the coaching session she was completely out of her depth. She was fearful of saying the wrong thing and further upsetting Bhavini.

Reverting to her linear coaching model, she asked Bhavini what outcome she wanted from the coaching that session? With a deep sad sigh, Bhavini suggested they could explore whether she should draw the line and break all ties with her friend forever. An hour later, having explored the issue, and gone around and around in circles, it was evident that there wasn't going to be a clear resolution to this in one coaching session.

Gillian, feeling a little frustrated that she wasn't achieving a result, asked the 'devil's advocate' question of whether someone joining a racist party due to anger and then leaving it meant they are really a racist. The question was left hanging in the air and Bhavini agreed she needed more time to think this over. This was the last session as Bhavini decided that coaching wasn't really working for her.

What could Gillian have done differently or needed to understand?

- Bhavini had just had a massive shock. All friendships and relationships form part of our identity so to discover that someone who has been a part of our life has hidden something so painful, is a devastating betrayal of trust. Asking to agree the outcome of the session was important but Gillian needed to let go of the linear model and flex from her typical challenging coaching style.

- Gillian should have spent a lot more time creating psychological safety and contracting around what is a highly sensitive coaching issue. Also, she might have agreed if it was ok to coach Bhavini on this area, as this was very different from their original agreement on career coaching.

- In the service of the coaching experience, Gillian could have shared how she was feeling about Bhavini's experience and how hearing her experience impacted her. She didn't have to use the words psychological safety, however; as long as she was not projecting her story or giving advice it can be perfectly acceptable to share. This assumes that Gillian had genuine empathy for Bhavini's predicament. Fake empathy or condescending sympathy would lack integrity and lose trust instantly with the client. In that case say nothing.

- Gillian needed to understand and show empathy that her client may be in grief and shock at the loss of a friendship she had treasured all her life.

- The devil's advocate question was wholly inappropriate and insensitive. This wasn't the appropriate occasion to test the strength of Bhavini's perspective by exploring an opposing view. Considering Bhavini's friend had defended her husband's reasons for joining the political party, and then avoided answering her when questioned about his harmful and prejudiced views, it could come across that Gillian had missed how deeply painful and sensitive this experience was for Bhavini from the perspective of both racism and personal betrayal.

- Coaching is about meeting the client where they are and not always about pushing them towards a goal or outcome. Gillian should have patiently given her client the time to process what had happened and allowed the outcome to evolve naturally.

It is important for coaches to understand that someone's experience of discrimination is complex; a reaction to a current event may have invisible roots to past experiences and may trigger strong emotions. Be prepared and open to hearing about the past too. Don't be tempted to shut the conversation down in pursuit of the goal and outcome.

HOW TO COACH SOMEONE FROM A MINORITY GROUP WHO MIGHT NOT BE FEELING PSYCHOLOGICALLY SAFE

Past and present experiences of discrimination are one of the many reasons someone can have an overall sense of feeling emotionally unsafe. Coaching is an opportunity to help clients build their psychological safety muscle and gain the confidence to speak up, to be seen and take courageous action. It is a powerful way of building healthy resilience and to tap into their creativity to make empowered decisions and choices.

Firstly, it is important to recognize behavioural clues which may be a sign that someone does not feel psychologically safe. Watch out for the following types of scenarios:

- Are they emotionally withdrawing from the situation or person?

- Are they physically withdrawing from the situation or person?

- Do they have a tendency to hide and not put themselves forward?

- Are they verbally aggressive and self-sabotaging?

- Are they turning down opportunities for self-promotion?

A lack of psychological safety may also result in a lack of confidence and vice versa. To focus on building confidence without acknowledging psychological safety could create a blind spot during coaching.

Instead, explore what or who needs to be in place to support your client in taking the steps towards 'feeling' safe. It is also worth exploring whether there are any patterns of scenarios which lead to someone not feeling safe. By pinpointing and understanding the roots of unsafety we can unpick and explore personal strategies for overcoming these.

The following is an excellent example of a powerful coaching scenario when issues of racism and microaggressions are surfaced and explored successfully.

CASE STUDY: NAIMA

Naima is a 32-year-old organization development consultant. She is a Muslim, French-born national of Moroccan heritage, living in the UK.

As part of her career progression, Naima's private sector organization offered her the opportunity to work with a coach. Following a 30-minute initial chemistry session, she started working with Jill, a highly experienced internal coach.

During one of their early sessions, Naima explored whether she should raise her hand and accept the opportunity to lead on a strategic initiative her organization was launching in the workplace to tackle racism. Following the COVID-19 pandemic, and the death of Black Americans George Floyd, Breonna Taylor and Ahmaud Arbery which led to the Black Lives Matter movement in June 2020 and worldwide protests across the globe, Naima was invited to volunteer as part of a taskforce to draft a strategy on racism. Having talked it through in the coaching session, Naima felt very drawn to the programme for several reasons. It would be an opportunity to work with very senior stakeholders in the business and, more importantly, the project was aligned with her core values. It made perfect sense for her to accept the invitation to get involved.

Initially, she felt flattered and excited to be involved in a high-profile programme; however, this feeling was short-lived and the experience of participating in the exercise was traumatic, complicated and distressing. Getting involved in the programme had meant she had to revisit her own personal experiences of racism and Islamophobia. Jill coached Naima through these experiences and was confident that their sessions were helpful and supportive.

A few months into the project, Naima was asked to share and present her findings to the wider senior leadership team. As soon as she started her presentation, she was met with awkward silences and a few disingenuous smiles. She felt patronized from the outset as all her suggestions were dissected, vilified and rejected. Someone in the room commented that the issues she was reporting were isolated and did not require further discussion. The lived experiences she was sharing were shockingly minimized or thrown out altogether. Others talked about how inclusion was more important than tackling racism as this meant other groups were left out. It quickly dawned on her that what the team were really asking for was a watered-down palatable report.

During the presentation, she had been the only minority person in the room. The diverse sponsor of the taskforce, a South Asian colleague, was absent on the day. She recalled it as her most psychologically unsafe experience in her career which left her feeling shocked, bullied, angry and highly upset. She was used to challenging conversations at work; only this had pushed one too many of her vulnerable hot buttons.

At the following coaching session, her coach Jill noticed a noticeable shift in Naima. She was not her usual polished, gregarious self. Instead, she seemed distant, vacant and somewhat withdrawn. Although she shared that the race project had de-railed, she didn't go into any more detail. It was obvious she didn't want to divulge any more and wanted to avoid the topic altogether. The coaching session felt disjointed and awkward.

The following session was a few weeks later and this time Naima shared more; however, it was clear to Jill that Naima was still holding back. Jill had a feeling that something monumental had happened to have completely quashed Naima's enthusiasm. She courageously asked Naima to share a bit more about what actually happened. On hearing her experience a few things came to Jill's mind.

By sharing her findings and speaking the truth Naima had experienced microaggressions and racism which had left her feeling psychologically unsafe and extremely vulnerable.

Working with Jill, as a white middle-class coach, Naima now felt afraid to share openly with her too during the coaching. Fearing a repeat of what had happened in the leadership meeting, this may have shut down the opportunity to have a meaningful coaching experience.

Although she had initially contracted around confidentiality this does not always translate across to the client automatically feeling emotionally and psychologically safe. She had to re-build Naima's need for psychological safety during coaching and beyond.

Jill needed to manage her own reaction to Naima's experience. This could be something she should pick up in her own supervision, ideally with a supervisory coach with an understanding of how to coach through a wider systemic lens.

A pivotal moment in the coaching was when Jill asked Naima how the experience had made her feel. This gave Naima permission to own what had happened to her and the courage to say out loud that the behaviour she had experienced was – from her perspective – unacceptable. Another powerful moment during the coaching was when Naima felt confident enough to use the word racism about what happened – it was important to allow Naima the opportunity to share how the experience had impacted her. This was her lived experience and if the coach denied it, will have the result of belittling and minimizing the coaching experience. Most likely Naima would relive the humiliation of not being believed.

Jill was patient and allowed Naima to share her experience and the consequences of how it had affected her emotionally and practically. A masterful coach, she had successfully created a safe container and within it nurtured a feeling of psychological safety through a fragile balancing act of empathy, trust, courage, respect and vulnerability.

Continuing their work together, Naima eventually decided to leave the organization on her own terms for a more senior role with a competitor.

An external unrelated event can trigger past experiences of feeling psychologically unsafe. If this does happen, it is important that the client is allowed to speak and share what happened without fear of being shamed or their experiences trivialized.

CASE STUDY: ORISA

Orisa, a 34-year-old financial consultant, is a British-born Nigerian with Greek heritage. Her early years were in Nigeria before returning to the UK at the age of seven to attend an all-girls prep boarding school.

We spoke shortly after the England football team lost to Italy during the Euro 2021 finals. Following the match, social media was inundated with a horrific storm of racist abuse hurled at three British-born black players: Marcus Rashford, Bukayo Saka and Jadon Sancho. Orisa, herself a passionate athlete and lacrosse player, was emotionally upset and very triggered by the event as it reminded her of her own past experiences on the sports field. At school, as a top performing athlete, on a number of occasions she too had been targeted and left feeling psychologically unsafe.

At the age of 12, Orisa attended an elite British boarding school. A very talented athlete at school, she wasn't offended or bothered by comments such as, 'You're faster because you're black' and innocently she let them pass. From her perspective, she was just very proud of the fact that she was the fastest in her school year.

But there was one time that stood out for her and still impacts her today. At 15, during a lacrosse match, she overheard parents from the opposing team who were getting frustrated that their daughters' team was losing. They had noticed Orisa's sporting prowess and saw that she was scoring many goals and easily the best player on the pitch. This led them to single her out and she overheard them discussing the 'black girl'. Orisa was the only black girl playing in the match that day and it was obvious they were talking about her. Throughout the match she heard the parents say, 'Get her! get her!'. Orisa recalls this making her feel insecure as she stood out and felt very psychologically vulnerable. The sickening feeling of being singled out by adults as a child and described by her colour has stayed with her.

Her other memory is of a classmate's parent who took her to one side and told her he could pretend to injure her so his daughter would win the race instead. At the time Oris brushed this off; however, in the long run this has also stayed with her.

At school, and on many occasions in adulthood, Orisa has felt psychologically unsafe. Every now and then, an event like the racism experienced by the footballers catches her out and she feels emotionally winded, vulnerable and deeply upset for days on end.

We discussed what she needed from a coach at a time like this. Her response was that she needed the freedom to express her emotions without feeling she was making a fuss or that she was just 'crazy'. Coaches need to understand that it takes courage to speak up and share this level of vulnerability. Enabling clients to share their experiences can have a profound positive impact on emotional wellbeing and health.

The important points to take away from the stories of Orisa and Sara in this chapter are that the seeds of feeling psychologically unsafe – despite privilege – are often planted in our childhood when we are at our most vulnerable and dependent on adults.

Coaching and vulnerability

Being coached can in itself leave some clients feeling very vulnerable. I know many clients from minority groups, who have been recommended for coaching, respond negatively with the initial reaction that it's because of underperformance rather than an opportunity to advance. These sessions typically start with the client asking for mentoring and consultancy. Being asked to share what's on their mind will leave them feeling very exposed and unsafe. There are also cultural sensitivities and generational differences about what is ok to share and what is not. In this instance, the coach has to go the extra mile by creating psychological safety through confidentiality and sensitivity. Rushing forward too quickly or asking too many direct personal questions may end up with a transactional superficial coaching session.

If there are certain situations where they withdraw, hold back or self-sabotage, ask your client to voice what is happening for them at that time.

One of the downsides of recurrent experiences of feeling unsafe is that we learn to avoid similar situations, not taking risks, not being creative and therefore limiting our potential. Sara is a perfect example of this. Playing small also comes at a price and can lead to unhappiness and feeling invisible and not heard. Some clients may find themselves in a no-win situation: they lose if they speak up and they are still losing by hiding.

At some point, they will need to make a conscious decision about what it means for them to live their best life. A coach who can create a psychologically safe environment can help someone who doesn't feel psychologically safe outside coaching to explore new ideas in a safe space. Coaches are not healers; however, being seen and being heard is a healing experience which can give someone the nudge to develop the confidence they need.

According to psychological research, a powerful way of overcoming psychological discomfort is to lean into the pain until the impact subsides (Crane and Searle, 2016). It means building a healthy resilience through gradual and managed exposure. For example, it could mean, if you need to have difficult conversations, pick your battles; gather your allies and surround yourself with the right crew while you build yourself back up again.

For a coaching conversation to be meaningful and transformational, clients need to feel safe to share what's on their mind as well as their lived experience. A psychologically safe and non-judgemental coaching presence is the most advantageous state for coaching. An attuned and present coach can foster a neuro-physiological state of safety, creating a container for the client to feel heard, championed and seen – feeling safe and courageous to have uncomfortable coaching conversations.

Each of us has a unique lived experience and many of us have become experts at shapeshifting – only to realize we have forgotten our true selves, become disconnected from our purpose and are striving to regain or hold on to some aspect of our identity. For many, the shapeshifting mask is how we keep ourselves psychologically safe.

I invite you to be curious and explore your client's strengths, fears and behaviours through the lens of psychological safety. When is your client thriving? What is happening around them?

Reflective work

Have you ever had to coach a client who shared an experience of when they were bullied or were on the receiving end of prejudice (this could be sexism, racism, homophobia etc.), leaving them feeling psychologically unsafe and vulnerable?

- What happened when you coached them?
- What did you learn from that coaching experience?
- What did you do well?
- What didn't go well?
- If you haven't yet had to coach someone who was feeling unsafe due to prejudice what would be your biggest concern?
- What support do you need to overcome it?
- Can you recall a time when you didn't feel psychologically safe?
- Do you remember what that felt like?
- Where in your body did you experience the emotion?
- How did you deal with the situation?
- How would you react today, if you find yourself in a similar situation?

References

Crane, M F and Searle, B J (2016) Building resilience through exposure to stressors: the effects of challenges versus hindrances, *Journal of Occupational Health Psychology*, 21 (4), 468–479, https://journals.sagepub.com/doi/abs/10.2307/2666999 (archived at https://perma.cc/N5BJ-CD8T)

Edmondson, A (1999) Psychological safety and learning behaviour in work teams, *Administrative Science Quarterly*, 44 (2), 350–83, doi.org/10.2307%2F2666999 (archived at perma.cc/HGA2-ZA8W)

10

Thriving

Navigating the landscape from surviving to thriving

If you do follow your bliss you put yourself on a kind of track that has been there all the while, waiting for you, and the life that you ought to be living is the one you are living.

JOSEPH CAMPBELL, *THE POWER OF MYTH*

Some people will naturally flourish and thrive in life, some may need to try harder and 'strive' but for others the only option or way of being is the hamster wheel of survival mode. On the surface they all may appear successful, goal-oriented and driven individuals. However, living life in endless strive or just survival mode with prolonged and excessive stress can lead to burnout and physical and mental exhaustion. One of the goals and gifts of transformational coaching is steering our clients towards feeling empowered, living their best life and mastering their power. The coaching supports them in moving forward by navigating their personal landscape from just surviving to thriving.

Personal enablers for thriving include:

- Feeling we are in control of our lives.
- Taking a positive outlook on life.
- Having a proactive personality.

- Feeling intrinsically and extrinsically motivated.
- Being committed to learning and expanding our knowledge.
- Feeling psychologically resilient.
- Being socially competent – that is, surrounded by family, friends, and colleagues.
- Having a healthy personal relationship with money and the definition of 'success'.

For those who are just surviving there may be life circumstances that have led to them feeling that they have little or no control at work or home. This modus operandi saps energy and can lead to a feeling that there is nothing more to give. This depletion can potentially manifest in long-term physiological changes, such as lowering of the immune system and increasing vulnerability to underlying or chronic ailments. Regardless of background, having some semblance of control in our lives and the decisions that impact it will lead to positive outcomes for wellbeing, performance and health. Even the most challenging circumstances can be more manageable if we feel that we have some say in the outcome, while the smallest of stresses can become magnified if the perception is one of complete powerlessness to change the situation.

> 'Exercising choice and the need for control – much like eating and hunger – are biologically motivated. While people may be biologically programmed to desire the opportunity for choice, the value of exercising specific choices likely depends on the available cognitive resources of the decision-maker in the given context, as well as the subjective value of the choice contents, influenced by personal experience and social and cultural learning.' (Leotti, Iyengar and Ochsner, 2010)

In both of the following case studies the individuals interviewed were very driven, ambitious, busy and highly capable people. This was what they wanted the world to see and what everyone around them actually did see. As their stories unfolded you will see that their façade of thriving was hiding the real-life experience of just trying to survive.

Read Aisha's story – a clash of cultures.

CASE STUDY: AISHA

Aisha works for a private sector organization as a coach, is 36 years old and describes herself as a British Bangladeshi Muslim. She is a single parent and lives in the East End of London. This is her story.

'When I was 16 years old, my parents pulled me out of college where I'd only been for just over one term, excited to study Chemistry, Psychology and Maths, to take me to Bangladesh.

Once we arrived in Bangladesh it was then they brought to my attention the trip was for the purpose of marrying my cousin. I lived in a very close community, and I had heard some of these rumours, but I was in complete denial my parents would do something like this to me.

Over the period of the next few weeks I continued to object against the situation but then finally gave in to the emotional blackmail that if I didn't marry then my parents would die of shame and the community would not be happy. My uncle's family were poor and I would be helping them in the long run as my cousin, after marriage, could get a visa to come to the UK, to find better work and be able to provide for them and me.

I reluctantly got married 14 days after my 17th birthday. I didn't consummate the marriage and continued to stay at my parents' house in Bangladesh. I had very little contact or communication with my husband and after a few months I came back to the UK.

When I returned, the length of time away from college meant I was unable to go back. The opportunity had gone and took away my desire to learn, to go to university and become a doctor.

The next few years I spent working two part-time jobs to raise the funds to show the Home Office I would be able to provide for my husband and keep a roof over our heads. At this point I feel I grew up pretty fast – I went into adulthood and took on the responsibility, alongside my dad, of providing for a household of six – while my friends finished college and went on to university, had social lives, were able to date, go out and enjoy being young.

In all this time I continued to have a minimal relationship with my husband. When he called from Bangladesh I didn't want to speak to him. Eventually the dreaded day came when he arrived in the UK. Everyone around me was happy and excited, and the household had a wedding atmosphere, but I was hiding behind my smile. I hated this and yet had to comply to keep my parents respected and honoured in society.

Over the next year this so-called marriage looked like a marriage on the outside – we both put on our smiles to face the community and family – but behind the closed bedroom doors we continued to be strangers. No conversation. Silently going to sleep and, on many occasions, faking being asleep so I wouldn't have to talk to him or go near him. He did force me to be intimate with him; it was like a transaction with no love or conversation.

While always being the pushover at home I had the opposite role in the workplace. I began to thrive, to grow and find my voice and I was looked to by other colleagues for direction and guidance. The impact of being acknowledged for what I could do and having my opinions valued grew my confidence and this slowly started to seep into my home life.

I began to realize it didn't matter that I was a dark-skinned girl, my opinions and my voice did matter and I shouldn't just accept what was 'best for the family'. I began to take a stand: a stand that hadn't previously been taken in my immediate family, in my wider family and one which wasn't the norm in the community or the culture I came from. I said I wanted a divorce at 20 years old.

I was scared. I knew there would be consequences and I feared what would happen next. I was right to be worried. I was identified as a bad role model for the siblings, bringing shame to the community, a bad influence on friends: my parents stopped talking to me and threatened to disown me. They took my husband into the family home after I told him to leave the house I had bought and we lived in.

I felt alone and used to cry on the commute to work then walk into the building with a smile to start work. It finally became too much and I ended up crying to one of my managers at work, saying I needed help as I didn't know how to deal with the pressure any more. She told me I was strong, and I could do this, most importantly for me at this time she said she, along with the wider team, would support me.

Eventually my family gave in and accepted what I wanted on the condition I supported my ex–husband to get a visa. This would give him the ability to stay in the UK permanently and then I could legally divorce him. This took a period of eight years.

How have your experiences impacted you in the long run?

At 17 years old I was a young girl who took on the responsibilities of not just her own family but needing to provide for her husband and his family too. When I was forced to get married, I was letting everyone else make decisions for me. But, by becoming an income earner, I was empowered by what I could do and realized how strong I was. By fighting to get divorced it helped/forced me to take control of my life.

The inability to control my home life fuelled the fire in my professional life to work hard and achieve what I wanted, in turn giving me the confidence and power to regain control of my home life.

After having such a traumatic experience, what I believed to be resilience and being strong also translated into living in survival mode. Survival mode is the only way I knew how to live and so it unfortunately seeped into my next relationship. This meant accepting another arranged marriage, because I felt unworthy of being able to meet someone myself. I didn't allow myself to be vulnerable to the man I was married to – resulting in an 'unreal' relationship, avoiding having those conversations that were needed. I distracted myself by over-working in order to prove my worth and creating an illusion of myself which I portrayed to the world but keeping my true self hidden behind many veils, afraid to show who I really was.

How has this manifested itself during coaching/being coached?

Before I started coaching, I thought my problem was the desire to progress and succeed at work but then it became an obsession – chasing every single vacancy that came up, burning out, work–life balance being non-existent. The constant rejections started to make me ask questions: maybe I'm no good, maybe I can't do the job, maybe my opinions aren't important…

When I initially started having coaching, I had a coach who missed the mark from the outset. She told me how she herself was on her third marriage and it wasn't a big deal that I was divorced twice. Her advice was to throw myself into dating. It was obvious that she had no idea that, from a religious and cultural perspective, putting myself out there and experimenting with dating wasn't straightforward. She was also struggling to understand why I wanted to stay close to a family or community that wasn't wholly accepting and open about my life choices.

I realized that my constant need for validation and recognition by others in the workplace actually started at home where I wasn't getting that recognition from my mother.

All the things I was being praised for at work weren't recognized or appreciated at home. To add to this, my mother and I have very different beliefs around parenting – this has become more apparent since I have had my daughter. In her eyes, and those of my community, I was a failure: a twice-divorced single parent. The fact that I could support myself financially was not seen by my mother as a positive thing. To her mind I should have been at home looking after my child.

Having said all that, even if I had the choice to move away from the community I wouldn't leave. Despite the challenges I love the fun we have as a family and I feel at home and a sense of belonging.

I eventually started to work with a coach from a similar cultural background. She helped me to see how courageous I was and had a greater depth of understanding of why, despite the challenges, I wanted to stay with my community. Also, due to her cultural awareness of our work together, the coaching was much more profound and transformational.'

WHAT DOES AISHA'S STORY TELL US?

The empowerment that she gained in her work life, away from the family and community influence, gave her the confidence and ultimately courage to ask to change her home life circumstances.

Her route to this freedom was through battling, striving and surviving. She knew no other way to live her life. In the same way that her work-life courage seeped into her personal life, the battle to strive for better seeped into her work life. This has had a detrimental effect on Aisha and kept her in survival mode.

The next stage of her personal growth is to be able to separate her objectives and channel her energy productively and not necessarily equally but to thrive emotionally and confidently well in both.

What does a coach need to understand about Aisha?

Aisha's situation is complex. Although she may show up for coaching with what appears on the surface as a straightforward coaching goal, there are many more layers which may surface during the coaching for deeper personal transformation. Assuming Aisha wants to go there during the coaching, or feels she can with the coach, the following factors all need to be taken into consideration.

- Aisha has courageously fought against her family and cultural system to get divorced twice and live life on her terms. She has stood up to tradition and broken many systemic and cultural rules she needed to follow to belong. Therefore, she risked rejection and being ostracized.

- Despite all this she is still very loyal to her family and cultural system of origin. A coach would need to respect or even be curious that, despite the emotional turmoil, her love and loyalty towards her family and culture remain strong.

- With personal growth, she may also be feeling guilty, as she has loosened some of her bonds to her cultural system. A part of her may also still feel torn between different systems.

- A coach needs to show empathy for her experiences and at the same time be non-judgemental about her cultural and family system.

- The work system has rewarded Aisha's tenacity, yet the family system is the opposite. Striving has had a pay-off, however it is coming at a cost. She isn't thriving and could eventually burn out.

- Aisha is very entangled within the rules of many systems. British Bangladeshi culture is very different from the culture in Bangladesh. It is important that a coach understands the generational differences and the importance played by money and gender roles as to who should be providing it. The lack of understanding may have been why Aisha's initial coaching experience was not a positive one.

- By marrying her first husband, who was from Bangladesh, she was helping his family and her wider family out of poverty. One of the rules of belonging in her family and Bangladeshi culture is that those who have emigrated help and support family members back in their country of origin. It was an important factor in Aisha's request for a divorce to be 'accepted' that she still honour this need to support her husband's family by obtaining a visa for her husband.

- Aisha has had many life experiences of feeling powerless and although she is very resilient, it is a dysfunctional resilience. She will have an overwhelming fear around losing control again.

- It is important that Aisha's courage should be championed. It is likely she may be too focused on striving for the next goal to acknowledge her strength and candour at taking control of her life.

WHY WE NEED TO TAKE INTO ACCOUNT 'THE MONEY STORY'

Our relationship with money is emotional and complex; it can result in guilt, shame, fear and hope. The way we relate to money and our attitudes is impacted by our childhood experiences and life circumstances. At a material level, money and 'wealth' are used by society as a measure of success. Those seen to have lots of money are perceived to be 'thriving' and those without as 'surviving'.

In Aisha's case, money was a big factor in who she married: as a commitment to elders to bring the next generation to the 'more prosperous' UK, enabled through marriage. Despite economic gains in adulthood, those whose parents struggled financially through low social class, or emigrated, may still have a complex money scarcity story.

A logical, rational-side perspective may know that the likelihood of living in extreme poverty is low, yet the scarcity emotional wiring and systemic entanglements can lead to self-sabotage, not taking risks or high levels of irrational anxiety around not having enough money to survive.

Here are a few examples of a 'money story' which may show up during coaching; from the lived experience lens of someone from a minority group or lower social class; these could be getting in the way of thriving.

- Feeling guilty about spending money on themselves or being too extravagant, especially if their parents had little time or capacity for self-indulgence or self-care.

- As adults, feeling overly protective of how hard their parents worked to give them the best start in life they could.

- Sending money back to wider family in their country of origin. Often the first wave of immigrants that move to a more prosperous country out of a sense of duty, obligation and guilt will send money back to their family back home, even if they have little themselves. If the family's circumstances back home improve, for many of the next generation there is still a systemic and moral duty to keep sending money back.

- Impacting decisions around risk-taking, particularly with career choices. Staying too long in a job with low satisfaction – even if leaving and getting a new job could pay more.

- Won't invest in personal development, such as coach training, as this is perceived as self-indulgent and a waste of money.

- Memories of feeling embarrassed or bullied at school for not being able to participate fully, for example in class trips or requiring free school meals.

- Feelings of resentment, contempt or judgement over people that it is perceived 'had it better'.

- Holding on to the limiting belief that hard work alone will lead to success.

How do you explore the money story in coaching?

Use these open questions to unlock the part that money plays in your clients' lived experience.

- What does having money mean to you?

- How would it feel if you never had to worry about money again?

- How do you feel about having no money?

- What did you learn about money as a child?

- How is the financial past impacting your present relationship with money?

- How does the future you envisage relate to money?

- What are the family rules about saving or spending money?

- Do you have any beliefs about money which are no longer serving you?

- Are there any benefits to not having much money?

Read Anne's story of survival on the poverty line.

CASE STUDY: ANNE

Anne was born in the 1970s, white British, lower working class, with an annual household income around £10–14k. Her home was mainly council/social housing around the UK. She says:

'At three years old I was living with my parents in our first privately-owned home with a lovely long garden and I remember spending time outdoors. At that young age I recall a sense of feeling happy and settled from previous months when we had typically been living in temporary accommodation. We ended up in the West Country and my father secured work as a bus driver, working evening shifts and my mother would be the home maker.

I clearly remember the day my dad collapsed in the bathroom, which was downstairs, and my mum had to climb through the tiny window from the outside to get into the bathroom to unlock the door and drag him out into a recovery position. I saw him lying motionless and I remember my mum saying that I needed to stay with my dad on the floor, keeping a watchful eye, while she ran to the neighbours to get help, call the doctor and ambulance – as we didn't have a phone at home. I don't really remember much of the details of what happened next, but I do know from that day onwards everything in our lives dramatically changed.

Shortly afterwards, my father was diagnosed with epilepsy which meant that he could no longer drive or work as in those days an epilepsy sufferer needed to have three clear years without having a seizure to be able to reclaim or hold a full driving licence. We soon had to sell the house as there was no income and, from then on, we lived in social housing.

By the time I was ten years old our family had moved ten times in the search for permanent work. We didn't have any disposable income as all of it went on basic needs and I remember the saying 'watching the pennies' being familiar. During that time, I observed other families who had more than others. I remember other kids on the estates we lived on having family holidays, days out and affording new clothes.

It is no surprise to me that my father, who desired to be the breadwinner, suffered with low mood and depression and this dominated the feeling at home during my early childhood and teens. My father's health continued to decline following further complications. My mother eventually found work and I took on additional responsibilities at 12 years old such as collecting my sister from infant school, shopping and cooking the family dinner each week night so my mum could hold down her job.

How did you deal with it at the time?

At the age of three, nearly four years old I just remember sitting there next to my father peacefully lying on the floor, unconscious, keeping an eye on him yet without recalling any specific emotion. I know I sensed that the situation was serious; I felt in some way helpless but knew I needed to keep a watchful eye on him if he regained consciousness. But I didn't really comprehend in those moments, and at such a young age, the magnitude of the situation.

At ten years old, having uprooted and moved home so much, I remember feeling different from other kids and alone, without any meaningful childhood connections or friendships. Education was a challenge as the standards varied so much from place to place, which meant that the experience was inconsistent, and teachers felt that I didn't really have great future prospects. I didn't venture out much and nobody really visited any of the homes we lived in that much either, as we were never there too long, so everything always felt temporary. I never felt stimulated or enjoyment of life as most of the focus was on supporting my dad and then my little sister. I know I always hoped that each time we moved things might become happier, although I always felt upset moving on from the place we had just previously settled in.

At the age of 12–13 years old we had surprisingly lived at the same address for three years, so I had more established friendships. However, the situation at home meant that I didn't feel like a typical teenager. I was not able to go out freely with friends after school or have a part-time job to earn my own money, as I had other responsibilities at home. I know I felt at times resentful and frustrated which later led to being rebellious and leaving school with no qualifications. At 16 years old I had no real future ambition or career prospects. It was only as I started work in retail at 18 years old that I was seen as having potential by others.

How have your experiences impacted you in the long run?

Looking back, I think my childhood experience has strengthened and shaped my character and resolve to forge a different and more positive path for myself. I'm deeply curious, adaptable and highly driven to do the best I can for myself and for others who are less fortunate – being inclusive and creating equal opportunity is important to me. I do have a tendency to back the underdog in most situations as that is typically how I have felt most of my life. I don't really take anything material for granted as I have seen that the things you work hard for can be taken away easily: most importantly, good health cannot be taken for granted and it should not be underestimated how impactful the repercussions can be. This combination has most definitely impacted me but it's not all negative. Although I do suffer from high anxiety, and some may say I am overly caring, my strength of character has played into having a successful career; one I could have never imagined possible.

How has this manifested itself during coaching/being coached?

I realized the impact of harbouring such low self-esteem from a young age and that potentially this was a result of transference from my parents' sense of self, due to society's judgement of epilepsy, unemployment and living in social housing. Added to this, I didn't have any external support networks to validate my worth or bring me out of myself: no long-term friendships and an inconsistent education manifested in the sense that I am not good enough, not educated enough.

I was always very harsh and critical to myself. Even when my career was going well, I didn't feel worthy and suffered acutely from imposter syndrome.

However, my drive to 'more than just survive' resulted in a hypervigilance against the fear of losing all I have worked so hard for: a desire to enjoy life and to help others less fortunate put what is important into perspective. However, I acknowledge that there have been significant periods where my drive was an 'overdrive' resulting in burnout. The irony that I was driving myself beyond my limits and causing a similar poor health scenario that had plagued my father was not lost on me.'

What does a coach need to understand about Anne?

Hypervigilance and low self-esteem can stop you from living the life you deserve. Anne has childhood trauma which needs to be understood and it would be prudent to raise this during the initial stages of coaching. She may also be unusually sensitive to the people and environment around her – this could result in taking time to feel safe and being able to 'open up'.

- Due to years of feeling judged by society, Anne may be oversensitive to someone's expression or tone and take it personally.
- Anne may be latching on to partial truths – for example how her family were perceived by others – and for her to feel psychologically safe during the coaching the coach needs to be sensitive to how this is approached.
- Anne may tend to catastrophize, expect the worst-case scenario and therefore be very risk averse. However, the threat Anne feels may not always be real as her brain is overanalysing and overcompensating to any sensory input.
- Her low self-esteem and self-worth may play out in her avoiding self-promotion or 'shouting out' about her work.

- Her resilience dial will be leaning towards dysfunctional resilience rather than healthy resilience.
- Anne may not be coachable in certain areas of her life, especially where it is rooted in childhood trauma.
- Anne's hypervigilance has been a gift to her as it means she is very alert to risks and can take pre-emptive action.
- As Anne's childhood story is linked to her parents' financial struggles there may be a money scarcity story lurking in the background. This may appear in coaching if she decides to change jobs or go freelance. It may be useful to do some coaching around her money story.
- Self-care is often missing in people who are in survival mode; activities that release endorphins, such as walking in the park and gentle exercise, can be calming and create space to explore the expectation gap between actual and perceived threat.

Coaching to thrive: what have we learnt?

The perception of feeling we have control, and the conviction to take action and exert control, can be altered as a result of our lived personal experience with control. Coaching a client to build their confidence and courage to feel empowered enough to take control requires empathy, patience and the coach's ability to create psychological safety. This was covered in detail in Chapter 9 on psychological safety.

> The concept that we all have total freedom of choice and the power to take control of our lives is far too simplistic. Some people have associated personal autonomy and individual rights with a Western cultural orientation that is not believed to apply or to be strongly held within non-Western societies. For example, some popular theoretical perspectives, generally grouped within the rubric of cultural psychology (Shweder and Sullivan, 2003), have contrasted Western and non-Western cultures along the dimension of individualism and collectivism.

> As in the case with Aisha, her loyalties to her family of origin and the cultural
> systemic rules have meant that although she was powerless in those systems
> she also has a strong sense of belonging. The dichotomy between Aisha's
> experiences of 'control' at work (under a 'Western' system) and in her family
> life is stark, clearly confusing but ultimately, when supported by coaching,
> empowering as it was the catalyst for achieving her goal.

In the case of Anne, her transitory childhood and limited opportunities to be able to act like a child had a significant impact on her sense of self. The constant relocation and lack of stability meant she was very inward looking, only having real relationships with her immediate family and therefore acutely feeling the judgement that society placed on their situation. Her story highlights the important role that external relationships, and being part of systems outside of the family, like education, have in raising self-worth and providing opportunities for personal growth … the kind of growth in which our natural ability to thrive will flourish.

Both Aisha and Anne have overcome hardship and made great strides in their lives. Similarly, their adversity is rooted in the hearts of their family and childhood story. Their current success is predominantly due to sheer hard work, determination and tenacity. The fire in their belly is a reaction triggered through fear and the fundamental human need to survive. Fortunately, the results have paid off as they are now both to a greater degree emotionally and physically safe. Their circumstances have given them the compassion and drive to want to help others. These are all honourable qualities. However, a question to ask would be about their own capacity for self-compassion and self-care?

On many fronts, the coping strategies they have used have proved successful. Despite the emotional energy and burnout, they will be highly resistant to letting go and trying things another way. Like a rubber band, they will be pulled back to the old habits of keeping going no matter what the cost. Their greatest fear is having to go back to feeling helpless again.

Coaching is a great opportunity for them to jump off their hamster wheels to pause and reflect: to evaluate and celebrate their accomplishments, and to take stock of how far they've come.

Adopting a strategy: 'pause and reflect'

There is a famous story of two fearless lumberjacks who took on a challenge to see who could cut down the most trees in a day. Both men picked up their axes and got to work. One tree at a time, they both skilfully cut down many trees. Halfway through the day, one of the men noticed that after the other lumberjack cut down a tree, he would take a short 10–15 minute break.

At the end of the day, they added up the number of trees each chopped down. The man who had taken the breaks had cut down more trees than the one who had just kept going. Bewildered, he asked, 'How is it that I took no breaks the whole day and you took a break after each tree and you cut down so many more trees than I did?' To which the other replied, 'It's true I was taking a break, but what you didn't see is that I was sharpening my axe every time I rested'.

The moral of the story is that to keep going, without pausing to reflect and recharge, is the same as carrying on chopping trees non-stop. It could be likened to 'just surviving' rather than taking steps that allow you to thrive. We can do less and achieve more by taking time out.

Reflective work

Have you coached someone who is very driven, ambitious, busy and highly capable? They feel compelled towards continually working very hard and long hours. Based on your work together they are in survival mode and not thriving. They may be missing out on quality time with family and friends. Their family story may be one of poverty or adversity. Perhaps in later life they've had financial setbacks due to their partner getting into debt, ill health or lost control in some aspect of their life.

- What did you learn about them during coaching?
- What happened when you coached a client in this situation?
- Having read this chapter, is there anything that you would do differently?
- Has any of this happened to you? If so, how did you deal with it?
- What did you learn from the overall coaching experience?
- What would you be concerned about in this situation?
- Would you know when to signpost towards counselling?
- And what about your own personal experience about control of your life choices?
- What are your thoughts if someone says they have no choice?
- Do you believe we always have a choice?
- Have you ever experienced a complete lack of control in a situation for a prolonged period of time? How did you cope?
- What would you do differently now – knowing what you do now?
- When you're low on energy how do you pull yourself out of it?

References

Leotti, L A, Iyengar, S S and Ochsner, K N (2010) Born to choose: the origins and value of the need for control, *Trends in Cognitive Science*, 14 (10), 457–63, doi.org/10.1016%2Fj.tics.2010.08.001 (archived at perma.cc/37TM-HS5N)

Shweder, R and Sullivan, M (2003) Cultural psychology: who needs it? *Annual Review of Psychology*, 44 (1), 497–523, doi.org/10.1146/annurev.ps.44.020193.002433 (archived at https://perma.cc/8AQF-PLN4)

11

Equity

Coaching for all to build a legacy of belonging,
inclusion and social mobility

There is always inequity in life. Life is unfair.
JOHN F KENNEDY, *NEWS CONFERENCE* (21 MARCH, 1962)

To successfully move to a more equitable working culture we need to recalibrate what we think of as 'fair'. It is not about all receiving the same 'solution' but what each of us needs to help us to reach the same level playing field, to thrive and achieve our potential.

A common theme from the case studies shared in this book – from the perspective of lived experience and intersectionality – is that if you are from an under-represented minority background there is a high likelihood you may have experienced subtle and explicit rejection for no justifiable reason or had to work extra hard to achieve the same results as your colleagues. These experiences inevitably have an effect – leading to low self-worth and low confidence. Transformational coaching for all is a powerful tool for improving and promoting equity in the workplace and beyond through personal development and self-awareness. It is an enabler for self-confidence, self-worth and self-leadership.

A fundamental premise underpinning coaching is that we always have to meet our clients where they are and create a safe space to give them what they need from the coaching session. This is based on the further assumption that all coaches are skilled in how to coach through the wider lens of inclusion, belonging and equity. Meeting our clients where they are requires having an insight and awareness of their lived experience of psychological safety, sense of belonging, exclusion, lack of power and inequity, as mentioned in previous chapters.

In an ever-changing society, with an increasingly diverse work-force, the ability to effectively support, motivate and nurture all employees is an essential target for organizations. Leaders and coaches must be given the framework, tools and training to foster a culture that embraces equity and promotes social mobility. Coaching through the lens of equity requires the ability to be curious, commit-ted and to establish trust and intimacy with the client to have honest and safe conversations about systemic inequities. Building the trust to have those conversations requires strengthening our own lifelong emotional intelligence and understanding of privilege.

Why is it important to acknowledge 'privilege' when identifying what is 'equitable'?

Most of us have a complex relationship with our own privilege or 'lack of it'. I recall a conversation with a friend whose childhood was spent growing up in a large, detached home in the leafy affluent suburb of Hampstead, north-west London. She had attended private schools and then a top university, yet her complaint was that she hadn't been as successful or had as glamorous a career as some of her peers, including her cousin. The reason she gave was that her aunt was the deputy head of a primary school and her cousin had the privilege of her mother's guidance during her early school years, lead-ing to a high-profile career in the United Nations in comparison to my friend's seemingly more mundane career as a senior auditor for a global accountancy firm.

Another example of 'misplaced' privilege was during a discussion with a team about why it is important that we explore how to increase the diversity in the coaching profession by training up more coaches from under-represented minority groups. A white middle-class manager, with a successful career background, vociferously shared that she too was a minority, as a divorced single parent she lacked certain privilege. She didn't believe it was fair or inclusive to have a targeted positive action approach that didn't include someone like her.

Both these examples are true in that from their perspective, compared to others in their circle, they feel they are at a disadvantage. Privilege has nuances specific to each person and as coaches our role isn't to judge their stories but to open the lens and provide context and ask why others may hold a different view. It is important for us as coaches to be curious about our personal relationship with privilege, to understand our own lived experience and acknowledge our own privilege.

Read Graham's story – privilege or lack of it can come in many forms and it is not always obvious.

CASE STUDY: GRAHAM

Graham was referred to me through a colleague. In his late 30s, he was well-dressed, professional, polite, intellectual, driven and ambitious. He was originally from Australia, now living in the UK. Graham was at a crossroads and needed to make a decision about whether to invest in an MBA or to climb the corporate ladder without one.

The person who had recommended me to Graham – an extroverted alpha leader – had spoken highly of our work together and was someone Graham respected. Despite the glowing references from his contact, I got the impression that Graham was somewhat sceptical about being coached. However, he was close to burnout at work and desperate for help. Having recently joined a global corporate tech company, he was feeling out of depth with the enormity of the task ahead.

During our initial chemistry session, I instinctively warmed to Graham and could sense he had a high level of integrity and a great sense of humour. He came across as sensitive, loyal, pragmatic and introverted. My instinct was that I needed to be very patient in allowing him to open up in his own space and time. We started our work together with psychometric profiling using a report called Hogan Assessments. I have found this a very powerful way to establish rapport with certain clients, who feel more at ease if they have a report we can explore together and is something they can analyse afterwards.

Very early on in our coaching work together it became clear that wanting to do the MBA was really about self-worth and Graham overcoming his fear that he wasn't as smart as his colleagues. He didn't actually want to invest his time and money on an MBA. However, he still had a burning desire for promotion and wanted to gain clarity over what he needed to do to become a senior director.

As we continued our work together, he opened up and shared that although he knew it was important to network to get ahead, he wasn't comfortable with small talk. He was very switched off by the typical male topics of 'football' and 'rugby' which in his opinion were boring and futile. He was very judgemental of boorish male behaviour and was fearful that, as he wasn't that type of person, this would ultimately hold him back. I could see his point of view yet also sensed he had limiting beliefs around what he described as small talk, influencing stakeholders and networking. We explored different ways he could initiate relationships with senior leaders and he agreed to ponder on this further.

We had been working together for several sessions when Graham opened up and shared a very personal story. He had previously, during the initial contracting, told me about his therapy a few years earlier and how it had helped. Instinctively, I had parked that knowledge and had a strong feeling he didn't want to speak about why he went into therapy. Now, Graham did open up about his childhood, sharing how it had been very volatile. Although he was born into a very comfortable middle-class family, his alcoholic father – an ex-army man – had been abusive and violent. Reading between the lines, the family had lost their home and Graham had felt the need to protect his mother and his younger siblings.

During our session, he also recalled a painful memory of being shouted out and humiliated by a teacher who didn't believe he was innocent over a small mishap. Behind his not liking small talk was a fear of being punished for speaking up, his lived experience was one where not only had his voice not been heard he had been severely punished for speaking up.

Graham himself joined the dots to the realization of why he often held back from joining in conversations. His avoidance of this was a turning point in our work together and it opened up the door to exploring and reframing his beliefs around how to build relationships at work. A light bulb moment for him was instead of feeling bored with small talk he could take the lead and find topics of mutual interest for both parties. Why shouldn't he be the one to drive the conversation?

Graham's lack of emotional safety, financial and educational privilege was a result of his lived experience of childhood instability and trauma. Through coaching, he made the journey from unconscious disempowerment to mastering his own power. Until our work together he hadn't consciously been aware that he was self-sabotaging his career success by hiding and playing small.

Takeaways from coaching Graham

- I worked with Graham over a period of twelve months, and it took many sessions before he truly felt safe enough to open up. Building his trust required patience and curiosity.
- Meeting him where he was was the key to unlocking the powerful work we did together. During the first few sessions the coaching was very transactional rather than transformational.
- Graham had made it clear that he didn't want to share the details of his childhood trauma. This was respected and in doing so it gave him the confidence and built the trust between us to open up further. Much of the powerful work on his self-development was happening in between our coaching sessions together. As our work together continued, I started to trust the process of what was happening and not get entangled in my own story of questioning whether I was a good enough coach!
- A consequence of avoiding 'the end of the workday pint with the lads' meant that Graham was also left feeling excluded and lacked a sense of belonging.
- Graham's childhood wasn't one of privilege and the knock backs were still haunting him. His parents had divorced following a violent episode. He had lost his home and I suspected he no longer spoke to his father.
- He didn't always feel psychologically safe – similar to Anne's story in Chapter 10 – he was always hypervigilant.
- Reflecting on Graham's story, we need to look at privilege from a holistic perspective and as coaches we have to treat each client as unique.

TO PROVIDE EQUITY WE HAVE TO ACKNOWLEDGE PRIVILEGE

The concept of privilege really came into its own in the late eighties, when Peggy McIntosh, a women's-studies scholar at Wellesley College, Massachusetts in the US, started writing about it. In the late 1980s, McIntosh initially wrote a paper titled *White Privilege and Male Privilege: A Personal Account of Coming to See Correspondences Through Work in Women's Studies*.

From this study (McIntosh, 1989) I have highlighted below a range of statements that cover different life experiences relating to privilege. How do they make you feel?

- If I should need to move, I can be pretty sure of renting or purchasing housing in an area which I can afford and in which I would want to live.
- I can turn on the television or open the front page of the paper and see people of my race widely represented.
- I can be pretty sure of having my voice heard in a group in which I am the only member of my race.
- I can go into a music shop and count on finding the music of my race represented, into a supermarket and find the staple foods which fit with my cultural traditions, into a hairdresser's shop and find someone who can cut my hair.
- I can be sure that if I need legal or medical help, my race will not work against me.
- Whether I use credit cards or cash, I can count on my skin colour not to work against the appearance of financial reliability.
- I do not have to educate my children to be aware of systemic racism for their own daily physical protection.
- I can criticize our government and talk about how much I fear its policies and behaviour without being seen as a cultural outsider.
- I can easily buy posters, post-cards, picture books, greeting cards, dolls, toys and children's magazines featuring people of my race.
- I can go home from most meetings of organizations I belong to feeling somewhat tied in, rather than isolated, out of place, outnumbered, unheard, held at a distance or feared.

How do the above statements relate to your life experiences? How do the above statements make you feel?

If you feel comfortable with some of these then consider what it must feel like for those to whom it does not apply. This inequity in society is only really felt by those where the statements do not ring true and yet, to create a more equitable society, those that do have the privilege need to understand what not having privilege feels like.

Privilege, guilt and shame

Facing into our own privilege can feel uncomfortable. Most of our privilege is acquired at birth and not through our personal choice. Feeling guilty and ashamed of our privilege can end up in paralysis of feelings and lead to inaction. As coaches, we are in a powerful position to make a change. Furthermore, having privilege doesn't eradicate our own life's twists and turns. Heartbreak, mental health, grief and loss can happen to any of us. Privilege should not stop anyone speaking their truth and asking for support and help.

Recognising the opportunity gap

As coaches we simply cannot ignore the reality and existence of the opportunity gap for many from under-represented groups who do not have economic and cultural access to the dominant, middle-class income experiences. It is well established that middle-class parents in the UK have the opportunity to access the postcode privilege of buying a house within the catchment area of a good school. In addition to this, they may also have the ability to pay for private tutoring and extra-curricular activities such as sport, drama and music. All of these can provide a 'leg up' for future opportunities and build self-confidence.

Privilege and psychological entitlement

Privilege with a sense of superiority and psychological entitlement is a well-established issue. Anyone who holds the belief that they deserve more and are entitled to more is a cause for concern. As Campbell et al note:

Psychological entitlement has been linked to a pattern of selfish and self-serving beliefs and behaviours – deserving more than others, greater game playing and less empathy (2004).

Entitlement can be misinterpreted as confidence, capability and the charming veneer of charisma. It is also a quality that not so long ago in some societies was revered. It is also often linked to self-absorption.

> As we reflect on elitism in the coaching profession, a worthwhile question is to recognize when our own sense of psychological entitlement is in the driving seat behind our need to affiliate and speak up about the on-trend newsworthy causes including diversity, inclusion and climate change etc.

A coach or leader who is in denial or defensive of their own privilege may find it challenging to connect and have empathy with a client whose background lacks privilege. To combat this, it may be an idea to spend time self-reflecting on why they are resisting to accept their own privileged position; in addition to this, asking themselves what aspects of their privilege have eased their life path. This could also be an opportunity for a positive gratitude exercise to acknowledge personal advantages.

Coaching for social change

From the outside looking into the coaching profession, specifically executive coaching and internal coaching pools in organizations, there are systemic inequities. The coveted thought leaders and power brokers who dominate the coaching space are predominantly privileged, white and middle-class. As with any system there are hidden loyalties and rules for belonging. In the next chapter I will address ways that the coaching profession needs to rebalance its own systemic inequity.

'Coaching as a social approach – especially with socially vulnerable individuals – has several implications: The foundation upon which the coaching contract is agreed has to be reviewed, the coaching process needs to incorporate elements to deal with issues of power, internalized oppression and social action, and the development of coaches needs to prepare them to face the unique challenges of that context.' (Shoukry, 2016)

Coaches need to have the skill of understanding and unpacking the systemic inequities which may be underlying a coaching scenario presented by a client vs an issue which lies with a client's personal story, mindset or limitation. In most circumstances, it is usually a combination of systemic challenges and someone's personal strategy for responding and coping in a system which is biased, or is not set up to support or promote their wellbeing and growth.

Consider the following scenario of two graduate interns at the end of their placement, applying for a full-time role for a global investment bank. As part of the final stage interview process, they need to do a presentation to a panel of leaders across the business. Both have been assigned coaches to help prepare for the interview.

One is privately educated and throughout his schooling has been exposed to debating societies, clubs and activities where he has had to stand in front of an audience and present. He found the internship enjoyable and was on two occasions invited out for client lunches to shadow a senior manager. One of the client's team at the lunch was an old family friend. Two people on the final interview panel are also alumni from his school. During coaching his biggest goal is to explore the content for the presentation and how he could make a great impression at interview. This is a straightforward coaching session and by the end he leaves feeling confident and prepared for his upcoming presentation. Although he is oblivious to the bigger picture, the banking system works to his advantage and the whole process is effortless.

The other candidate is from a working-class background and was the only person from her school to attend a prestigious university. Throughout her internship, with some managers she has struggled to make a good first impression. Not entirely at ease with the very 'male' culture and office banter, she often chose to go out for a walk at lunch to avoid socializing. Through the grapevine she found out the other candidate was being invited to client lunches and this made her feel even more insecure and that she wasn't good enough. To overcome this, she decided to work harder and longer hours to prove her worth. One of her managers had jokingly hinted she needed to take things less seriously. During coaching she wanted to focus on building her confidence.

In this situation, a coach would need the wider angled systemic lens to understand, empathize and acknowledge the systemic challenges she is facing and not just place the focus on building her confidence. Behind the lack of confidence there are hidden systemic issues of prejudice towards someone from her socio-economic class, gender and educational background. A recognition of these – on top of a sense of not belonging and exclusion – may have further impacted her confidence.

It may be worth exploring how she feels about the culture at the bank? What is working? How is it different from what she was expecting? What does she find challenging? What makes her unique? The coaching would be an opportunity to navigate and explore her personal power while accepting that there are systemic challenges – building her confidence from a place of power rather than as some part of her that needs fixing.

A coaching process that supports social change would need to consider several aspects. First to consider its power. Socially vulnerable clients are likely to be more susceptible to the effect of power dynamics. Differences between coach and client, in terms of gender, race, class and other factors, may significantly add to the complexity of power in the coaching relationship. Nevertheless, 'Power flows in both directions, as coachees contribute through active consent or resistance' (Jones, Armour and Potrac, 2002).

Despite identical goals, both interns had very different needs from the coaching to help them prepare for their final presentations. For exemplary coaching to be accessible to all, we need coaches who are masterful at recognizing systemic nuances with the tools and skills to have bold coaching conversations.

Systemic inequities and feeling less than everyone else

Now read Hema's story; feeling lesser than someone else can elicit a sense that we always have to 'fight' to be heard. This is a state which over time can leave us feeling emotionally and physically exhausted.

CASE STUDY: HEMA

Hema is a British-born Hindu, in her early 40s, a senior civil servant and experienced coach. She is married with two children. She shared how during a self-reflective exercise during her coach training she had the light bulb moment of why she often felt she had to fight for her voice to be heard.

'I recall a memory that made me realize and understand some of the inequalities that I may feel. With our birthdays a week apart, my brother and I had a joint birthday party, it was his first birthday and my third. Coming from a large Asian family we had loads of people in the house, we had a big cake and the cake was divided into two halves, blue for him and a pink half for me. Everyone was just interested in him as it was his first birthday. And then when it came to cutting and blowing out the candles, all the attention was on him. And I guess at that time, I just got upset because all the candles including those on my side were blown out by him and I didn't get a chance to blow my own candles on my cake.

That's probably where it all started, I didn't even get a look in. It feels quite trivial to be bringing it up. But it makes sense and explains why I always feel I need to not assert myself, but always just make sure my views are heard.

How has this translated into the workplace?

'I don't like to work within boundaries. I like to take risks. I like to play devil's advocate. I like to be creative and innovative. If I'm doing a role, I need to do something that's quite creative – I need to look outside of the box. And that's the only way that this piece of work is going to be – I need to be praised, I need it to be recognized. Although it is great to be creative and going above and beyond, there is quite a bit of firefighting to achieve this, just for the need to be seen. All of which is emotionally exhausting and often leaves me depleted.

I think it's a response to not being seen – not being heard. I was going through life this way, but then during my coach training, it helped me go back to almost the source of why I am the way I am.

At home, I always feel I'm in my brother's shadow. You see the inequalities of being treated in a particular way as a daughter.

When I got married, in my husband's family, I was told the women have always observed a fast called 'Karwa Chauth' which they do to ensure their husbands live a long and healthy life. The sentiment behind this ritual was completely at odds with my belief and values. Until recently, although I didn't agree with it I did it to keep the peace. Ours wasn't an arranged marriage, we had dated and chosen each other. Also, I felt additional pressure as I had married someone from a different caste. I felt I needed to go the extra mile and make an effort with my in-laws. My husband is loyal to his family and wanted me to fast as he'd grown up seeing his mum do the same, regardless of my needs and wants in the relationship.

The fasting had taken me back to feeling controlled and governed by a set of rules and protocols. You're told when you get married you can do what you want but actually you're then expected to live by another set of rules. Those set by your husband's family. Because we chose each other I thought I was going into the marriage with autonomy and my voice would be heard. So again, not having that was uncomfortable.

One of my self-care tools is meditation and yoga. I know this may come across as a cliché for a coach; however, I find it helps me to connect with my inner wisdom and creativity.'

Takeaways from coaching Hema

- There is systemic inequity and entanglements in both her professional and personal systems.
- Hema's strength is her ability to think outside the box to make things happen. She has used this to her benefit and is a highly respected coach and employee.
- Hema may have unconsciously or consciously acquired a limiting belief that 'fighting' is the only way she will ever be heard.
- Always having to 'fight' to be heard could potentially lead to burnout and is emotionally exhausting. The emotional energy spent on 'fighting' is stressful and prolonged exposure to stress could have an adverse effect on her ability to think clearly, reducing her decision making, sociability and an openness to new ideas. She may find herself saying or acting in a way that will feel out of character and detrimental.
- As Hema is a coach, and has done the work on herself, she has a high level of self-awareness about emotional needs and capacity for self-care. There are scientific studies proving that meditation can positively impact us socially and emotionally (Tang, Hölzel and Posner, 2015).

How can we coach with equity?

How can we as coaches and leaders support marginalized under-represented groups who don't feel heard?

It is normal that we see the world from our lens and perspective; it is also predictable that we may have a blind spot about our personal privilege. On the flip side of this it is impossible for us to absorb and process every bit of information which is out there. This is confirmed in the psychological theory of 'bounded awareness' that we fail to see and use information that is easily available to us (Chugh and Bazerman, 2007).

However, as coaches we must be curious and open up to new voices or those that might not resonate with our own – understanding what and why they have formed an opinion that may seem so different from ours. The better understanding we have of why someone holds a point of view, the better equipped we are at supporting others who have experienced the same.

> As coaches, we need the range of voices and the many different narratives that belong to individuals and groups to be foregrounded, to be present in our thinking, and to help us to extend the boundaries of our understanding and effectiveness. Tapping our own experience and making sure that we're exposing ourselves sufficiently to learning from the experiences and stories of others, can lead us to a broader, richer, clearer and more complete understanding of the racialization of experience and the impacts of race inequity. (Tawadros, 2021)

Reflective work

A few years ago, a close friend was diagnosed with a critical illness. I had never heard of the condition until her diagnosis; however, for the next few months at every turn I seemed to be bombarded with information about this illness: from the random article in a magazine that I came across at the hairdressers to a TV documentary. The sudden overexposure wasn't by chance, the information had always been there; however, as it didn't have any personal relevance, I just hadn't paid it any attention before my friend was ill.

Use the following questions to explore your understanding of privilege.

- Compared to someone from an under-privileged minority group, in which areas of your life have you experienced privilege?

- In what aspects of your life do you feel you lack privilege?

- How do you feel about coaching someone who has had a less privileged life than you?

- What would be your concern about coaching someone who has had less privilege than you?

- How do you feel about coaching someone who has had a more privileged life than you?

- What would be your concern about coaching someone who has had more privilege than you?

- What do you understand as the difference between equity vs equality?

- What can you do to improve your awareness of inequity and privilege?

- What action (big or small) can you take to stand against inequity and privilege?

References

Campbell, W K, Bonacci, A M, Shelton, J, Exline, J J and Bushman, B J (2004) Psychological entitlement: Interpersonal consequences and validation of a self-report measure, *Journal of Personality Assessment*, 83 (1), 29–45

Chugh, D and Bazerman, M H (2007) Bounded awareness: what you fail to see can hurt you, *Mind and Society*, 6, 1–18, DOI:10.1007/s11299-006-0020-4

Jones, R L, Armour, K M and Potrac, P (2002) Understanding the coaching process: a framework for social analysis, *Quest*, 54 (1), 34–48

McIntosh, P (1989) White Privilege: Unpacking the Invisible Knapsack, *Peace and Freedom Magazine*, July/August, 10–12, psychology.umbc.edu/files/2016/10/White-Privilege_McIntosh-1989.pdf (archived at perma.cc/42LT-D536)

Shoukry, H (2016) Coaching for social change, in *The SAGE Handbook of Coaching,* ed T Bachkirova, G Spence and D Drake, pp 176–91, Sage Publications Inc, London

Tang, Y-Y, Hölzel, B K and Posner, M I (2015) The neuroscience of mindfulness meditation, *Nature Reviews Neuroscience*, 16, 213–225

Tawadros, T (2021) Inform your perceptions, Part 3, *Coaching at Work,* July, www.coaching-at-work.com/2021/07/01/inform-your-perceptions/ (archived at perma.cc/RD6E-69RC)

12

Allyship

Open letter to organizations committed to creating an inclusive coaching and mentoring culture

I speak – not for myself, but so that those without a voice can be heard.

MALALA YOUSAFZAI, UNITED NATIONS SPEECH (JULY 2013)

Talent is everywhere – but opportunity isn't. Inclusive hiring isn't enough. Employees from socially disadvantaged backgrounds are left behind as they face many systemic and cultural barriers to career development. Embedding a coaching culture with access to coaching for all can open up purposeful and meaningful pathways for progression.

The benefits from being coached are endless: self-awareness, empowerment, gaining clarity, achieving goals, leveraging strengths, confidence, acquiring new ways of thinking, learning new skills, motivation, understanding others, feeling supported, navigating difficult decisions, overcoming hurdles, building relationships etc. Offering quality professionally trained coaching to *all* makes perfect business sense.

Yet, in most organizations, coaching is usually only offered to those in senior positions and, due to a lack of representation in senior positions, this excludes many from under-represented minority groups. Even when these groups are offered a coach, unless the coach has the skills and self-awareness to create trust and psychological safety by coaching through a wider lens of inclusion, belonging and equity, there is a likelihood of their coaching being superficial.

Observing the coaching profession through a systemic lens

From the outside, the professional coaching industry consisting of executive coaches and internal coaches is dominated by middle-class women. Many of the power brokers and gatekeepers who are considered thought leaders in the coaching space are also 'privileged' white, middle-aged men and women. It is obvious that if the goal is to create equity and fairness in the workplace and wider society, we need coaches from a variety of socio-economic, cultural and religious backgrounds and coaches who understand the complexity of coaching through a wider lens of inclusion, belonging and equity.

Yet, as with any systemic change, the desire to keep things just as they are, is powerful. Each system has hidden systemic loyalties and rules for belonging. The coaching profession is not an exception and it will take time for things to change.

Allyship in increasing diversity of coaches

Those in positions of power and privilege can support these changes intentionally by taking action and by being an ally through investing in the training and development of diverse coaches. A great starting place for building a pool of diverse coaches is through internal coaching pools. The coaching profession needs a diverse and inclusive pool of attainable role models who will lead the way in making a difference.

Organizations such as the Co-operative Group and the British Transport Police have been pioneers in actively promoting and increasing the diversity of their coaching pool.

Many more organizations are investing in training managers and leaders with coaching skills. This is a great opportunity to embed their coaching skills within a wider systemic lens of inclusion, belonging and equity.

It is also important that organizations are mindful of internal coaches who are not committed to the deeper work of coaching, otherwise those who are not receiving regular supervision may inadvertently be offering very poor coaching experiences.

Why we need 'good' role models in coaching and mentoring

I recall an alarming conversation with a mature professional black woman who had been nominated as a participant for the Mastering Your Power coach training programme. Within a few minutes of our chat, she very innocently told me, 'I didn't think people like us could be coaches'. She wasn't the last person to share a similar sentiment. Her words stayed with me for many days afterwards: it was confirmation that there was much work to be done to shift the current inertia around increasing diversity in coaching pools in today's predominantly middle-class elitist coaching profession.

Many organizations are on a mission to build more diverse talent pipelines, with coaching, mentoring and reverse mentoring as popular approaches. This trend will no doubt continue to gain momentum. Many of the issues and coaching skills we have touched on in this book are equally applicable to mentoring too. However, it is important that mentoring and coaching are not bundled together as there are stark differences between the two.

A mentor shares their knowledge and experience to guide an inexperienced colleague whereas coaching is non-directive. In the last few years, there has been a momentum for coaches to be accredited and professionally trained, which is not the case with mentoring. Organizations can take very different approaches to running mentoring programmes, which can mean that the results of these schemes are variable too as many of the skills of mentoring overlap with coaching, such as questioning, active listening and building trust. It is important that all mentors are also trained to create psychological safety, rapport and are equally compassionate and empathetic.

Choosing mentors and coaches with care and due diligence

Consider the case of a positive action programme at a global financial services organization. The BAME mentoring programme was designed to match BAME junior and senior employees. The programme was launched without any training for the mentors nor any consideration for the importance of 'mentor and mentee' chemistry.

A 21-year-old black female IT graduate was matched with a senior South Asian female IT manager in her late 40s as her mentor. Both were placed together as they were minority women. The mentor, herself from a working-class background, had worked her way up to a mid-level leadership position. Many years ago after graduating, she had initially wanted to work for a global US tech company, however had failed to secure a place. Instead, she had worked in a number of public sector roles before landing her dream role with a significant pay increase in the IT department of an investment bank through a friend. Here she thrived in the pressurized culture and had moved around every few years. Even though each role had a pattern of toxic bosses and ended acrimoniously, she always moved on to the next one and both survived and thrived. When her organization offered her the opportunity to mentor she was delighted to jump in to show off her knowledge and help someone at the start of their career. However, the mentoring was not as she had expected. She found her mentee closed, withdrawn and disengaged. The mentee did not take her advice and the whole experience was not what she had expected. In fact, she started to worry that it would make her look bad in front of her bosses and to cover her back she made it known that the mentee was a poor hire. The mentee on the other hand was overwhelmed by the working culture and did not feel she was benefiting from the mentoring sessions. She struggled to connect with her mentor who often cancelled their sessions at the last minute. When they did happen, she found her mentor was dismissive, curt and condescending. Not surprisingly, the mentoring was a failure and the mentee left the organization.

It simply is not enough to match two people just because they are both from under-represented minority groups. Not only was the mentor untrained, she was a poor listener, lacked empathy and created no psychological safety. Her sense of self was one of superiority and a belief that, 'If I had to struggle to get to where I am so should you'. There was no guarantee that training in mentoring and coaching skills would have led to a better outcome; however, it would have been an opportunity to flag that someone may not be a natural mentor or coach.

Someone from a minority group who has assimilated (intentionally or unintentionally) the norms of the majority group to co-exist may feel uncomfortable at having to address the roots of their own cultural identity and therefore struggle to mentor someone whose issues are a projection of a past they want to forget.

Coaching skills training

The scenario with the mentor and mentee may have been avoided if the mentor had been a fully trained coach too: specifically, a deeply transformational coach training programme, where the training is a personal journey of self-awareness and personal development as well as coaching tools and models, could have been beneficial.

To support others fully in a heart-centred way we need self-awareness and to have done our own work too, recognizing that we are all on our personal ongoing journey of discovery and growth. A trained coach or mentor would know how to create psychological safety in the session. They would practise active listening to understand and explore the real issue holding the person back. They would also have a level of self-awareness of how they themselves are showing up during the session, therefore not allowing their own limiting beliefs, superiority or ego to negatively impact the work and relationship.

Where coaching has the upper hand over mentoring

There is immense wisdom in the phrase, 'Give a man a fish, and you feed him for a day. Teach a man to fish, and you feed him for a lifetime'. Mentoring is giving someone guidance that will help them with what they need at that time, however, the benefits of transformational coaching, especially if they open up a new perspective, overcome a limiting belief or connect with a deeper purpose and fulfilment, can have a ripple effect beyond the immediate coaching intervention. As organizations move towards a coaching culture, a diverse pool of coaches is valuable and necessary.

OTHERING

'Othering' is a very real phenomenon, which lies at the heart of much of the conflict in the modern world. We see many examples of minority communities being dehumanized and treated barbarically by the communities or groups who hold power. Othering, through deliberate misinformation and stoking of resentment and fear, is sadly a deliberate strategy of governments around the world.

This sounds simple but belies the complexity of group-based identity theories and the interweaving of deep-rooted wired behaviour and social construct. In recent years, neuroscience has shone a light in explaining some of the evolutionary reasons why othering is inevitable, as has behavioural economics.

Our worlds are incredibly complex, and it is estimated we have between 20,000 and 70,000 thoughts a day. Our brain takes short cuts, creating 'heuristics' or patterns, based on often incorrect assumptions and biases. And these cognitive processes underpin the concept of 'ingroup' and 'outgroup'.

The ingroup is the group to which we psychologically feel a sense of belonging. This served us well when we were living in caves and connection in the group and fear of neighbouring communities offered evolutionary advantage. Neurobiology plays its part; for example, when we perceive difference, the brain triggers the release of cortisol, the stress hormone.

One of the main problems with ingroup-outgroup thinking is the occurrence of outgroup homogeneity. We humanize those in our ingroup, recognizing their individuality, whereas we tend to assume all those in the outgroup are the same and we attribute common or group characteristics to them. All too often these applied characteristics are negative and this in turn drives the practice of othering. This leads to individual discrimination, but also to more systemic structural unfairness and inequity in how societies are organized.

So, if othering seems inevitable, what hope is there?

There is no easy answer, but the antithesis of othering is, in my view, belonging. How can we collectively create communities where the default is to approach others with love and actively focus on their humanity? We know segregation doesn't work, and assimilation robs people of their unique history and cultural identity, so maybe the creation of an inclusive society where everyone feels they belong is the goal we should be striving towards. (*Othering: A Perspective*, Rita Symons, not yet published.)

Internal coaching pools need a communication and marketing strategy

Over the years, I have sat through many conversations with close friends and family who have politely poked fun at coaching; telling me that coaching is nothing more than a chat or giving someone friendly advice. Their attitudes change when they are assigned a coach through their work, and I see a gradual shift of appreciation and pride for the work I've been doing for almost two decades.

What is a cause for concern is that in many organizations employees are assigned coaches to rectify underperformance (or most likely make up for weak management and leadership!). To be sent for coaching is potentially interpreted as a sign of failure or a last resort to attempt salvage a difficult employee situation.

Even if the coaching intervention is not because of under-performance, if someone is nervous about opening up they may initially feel uncomfortable or be defensive. If we consider this through the lived experience of someone from an under-represented minority group, who may have a complex relationship with psychological safety, inclusion, belonging and authenticity, to be offered coaching may elicit a plethora of negative emotions.

Anyone who feels that they were sent for coaching because they are 'not good enough', will hold back, feel unsafe and won't easily open up to or trust the coach. A common pattern is that they may ask for advice as they believe they have a knowledge gap and are missing information they now need to acquire. If they are used to wearing a virtual mask or editing which bits are ok to share at work, it may take several sessions to get to the point if and when they open up.

Many people I have worked with who have access to internal coaches at work routinely ask me to introduce them to someone outside their working environment. Despite reassurances over confidentiality, they still do not feel it is safe to be completely open and transparent with someone in their own organization. I don't expect the trust and confidentiality issue of internal coaches to disappear completely. However, it raises a red flag of how safe people feel about opening up with internal coaches.

Organizations need to be mindful of how coaching is marketed and perceived in the wider organization. They also need to ensure that their internal pool of coaches are all trained to coach through a wider systemic lens (beyond linear models) and are offered regular supervision. Crucially, coaching must be marketed as a positive opportunity for professional growth and personal development.

Coaching supervision

With transformational coaching as a professional discipline, we need to offer coaches supervision more often – beyond training courses and accreditations. Coaches need to incorporate integrity, quality and continuous professional development. Ongoing coaching supervision is pivotal for safeguarding and ensuring coaches also have an opportunity for their own personal reflection and growth. Coaching supervision must also incorporate the wider lens of inclusion, diversity, belonging and equity. Coaches need a safe place to share if they are struggling with a coaching intervention which feels too unfamiliar or if a client's system and values are very different to theirs.

Coaching and AI (artificial intelligence)

I am always in favour of embracing change and technology. However, when I consider the trend and movement towards AI in coaching, specifically from the perspective of the issues that have been raised in this book, I have major concerns. AI and coaching is certainly a cost-effective approach to championing accessibility of coaching for all. However, a question any organization considering this option needs to ask is, 'Are coaching bots and coaching apps fit for purpose if the data used to design the AI coaching tool is poor or biased?'.

MACHINE LEARNING

Machine Learning (ML) draws on data to come to a conclusion.

> The greater the quantity and diversity of data used to train, the better the quality of outcome. For this to happen we need a large diverse pool of experienced masterful coaches conducting live coaching sessions with a diverse pool of coachees. This rich data can then be used to design a robust, inclusive, emotionally intelligent and unbiased AI coaching tool. Currently, we are already off to a false start as there is a distinct lack of diversity in the coaching profession. If a young black female from a working-class background is offered AI coaching, how likely is this tool to produce the best outcome for her? (Isaacson, 2021)

The likelihood of bias is high: 'fixing discrimination in algorithmic systems is not something that can be solved easily' (Selbst et al, 2019) 'It's a process ongoing, just like discrimination in any other aspect of society.' A study done by the MIT Media Lab showed that facial recognition systems, on average, had a 35 per cent error rate when identifying the gender of dark-skinned females, compared with a 1 per cent error rate for white males (Buolamwini et al, 2018). This problem could be solved with a more diverse database, which would then train the system to accurately identify the genders of all people, regardless of skin colour.

It is most likely that AI coaching tools will be offered to those on the lower rungs of the organization or those at the start of their careers. For those from under-represented minority groups this may end up being their only opportunity for coaching. The potential benefit is likely to be very superficial if it is not followed up by a quality in-person coaching experience.

Team coaching through the lens of inclusion, belonging and equity

Team coaching is an exciting growth area for the coaching profession. We need to ensure that team coaches have the presence and compassion to stand in the truth of a system. I would urge a team coach to be mindful and aware of the dynamics of psychological safety, inclusion and belonging from the lens of someone from an under-represented minority group. Understand the impact of micro-aggressions and how these may be playing out in a team coaching session. Check in with a wider lens of the team dynamics of who is not seen and who is not heard. Be curious about how this plays out. Find the courage to ask the question. This book has many examples of the lived experiences of under-represented minority groups. Use this knowledge support you in team coaching work too.

Team coaches also need to understand the dynamics of inclusion, belonging and equity in coaching. Furthermore, we need diversity in the pool of team coaches as well, so that their perspective and observations can be brought to benefit teams.

And finally

We need to give diverse voices the platform to talk about why we need to see diversity in the coaching profession. These voices and their stories need to be celebrated, heard and respected

The secret source of coaching with a wide-angled lens of inclusion, belonging and equity is LISTENING deeply and intuitively.

Checklist and calls to action for coaching in organizations

- Does your organization have a mandate to retain and develop a diverse talent pool?
- Could coaching play a part in achieving this?
- Is coaching offered to *all* employees or a select few? If so, who and why?
- How diverse is your internal coaching pool?
- Are all your internal coaches capable of coaching through a wide lens of equity, belonging and inclusion?
- Do your coaches understand what microaggressions are?

- Are your coaches anti-racist?

- How comfortable are your coaches coaching someone from a different socio-economic, cultural and religious background?

- Does your organization have a community and marketing strategy for coaching?

- How is coaching perceived by all your employees?

- How is coaching perceived by employees from under-represented minority groups?

- How diverse are the external executive coaches you work with?

- Are the right people selected to be trained as coaches?

- Are your team coaches trained to coach through a wide-angled lens of inclusion, belonging and equity?

- Is the coaching supervision offered to the internal coaching pool through a wide-angled lens of inclusion, belonging and equity?

- How can you be an ally to coaching with a wider lens of inclusion, belonging and equity?

References

Buolamwini, J, Gebru, T (2018) Gender Shades: Intersectional Accuracy Disparities in Commercial Gender Classification, *Proceedings of machine learning research conference on fairness, accountability, and transparency*, 81 pp. 1–15

Isaacson, S (2021) *How to Thrive as a Coach in a Digital World*, Open University Press, Maidenhead

Selbst, A D, Boyd, D, Friedler, S A, Venkatasubramanian, S and Vertesi, J (2019) Fairness and abstraction in sociotechnical systems, in *Proceedings of the conference on fairness, accountability, and transparency*, January, pp. 59–68

INDEX

Note: Page numbers in *italics* indicate figures or tables